WESTMAR COLLEGE LIBRARY

P9-DGJ-786

The Firm and the Formless
Religion and Identity in Aboriginal Australia
Hans Mol

Religion and Identity: Social-Scientific Studies in Religion, 2
Hans Mol, editor

This volume is woven around the idea that wholeness (the firm) and fragmentation (risking formlessness) alternate in human affairs. This theme is applied to the history and the present condition of Australian Aboriginals. Their religion is seen as a way to bolster a precarious identity and to affirm order in an existence which would otherwise become formless. It deals with totemism as a form of ordering a variety of often conflicting identities. The author describes the modern predicament of Aborigines in Australian society and concludes that their revitalization will occur only when they manage to make economic self-sufficiency subordinate to a viable and firm view of existence. He critically integrates into his analyses and interpretations the positions of such well-known scholars as Frazer, Durkheim, Freud, Lévi-Strauss, Radcliffe-Brown, Eliade, and Stanner. The volume will be of interest to students of sociology, anthropology, and religion.

Hans J. Mol holds the Ph.D. degree in sociology from Columbia University, New York. He has held academic positions in New Zealand and Australia and is now professor in the Religious Studies Department of McMaster University. His best-known books are Religion in Australia, Western Religion, *and* Identity and the Sacred.

The Firm and the Formless

Religion and Identity in
Aboriginal Australia

Hans Mol

Wilfrid Laurier University Press

BL
2610
M642

*Religion and Identity: Social-Scientific
Studies in Religion, 2*
Hans Mol, editor

Canadian Cataloguing in Publication Date

Mol, Hans, 1922-
    The firm and the formless
(Religion and identity ; 2)

Bibliography: p.
Includes index.
ISBN 0-88920-117-X

1. Australian aborigines — Religion.
2. Australian aborigines — Ethnic identity.
3. Mythology, Australian aboriginal.
I. Title. II. Series.

BL2610.M64   306′.6   C82-094461-0

Copyright © 1982 by Hans Mol

Published by
WILFRID LAURIER UNIVERSITY PRESS
Waterloo, Ontario, Canada   N2L 3C5

82 83 84 85 4 3 2 1

Cover design by Michael Baldwin MSIAD

*No part of this book may be stored in a retrieval system, translated or reproduced in
any form, by print, photoprint, microfilm, microfiche, or any other means, without
written permission from the publisher.*

101720

Contents

Preface

This study has two purposes. The first one is to answer the question, "In which ways has religion reinforced the identity of Australian Aborigines?" That question is part of a larger research programme which deals with the "fit" (or lack of fit) between the identity model of religion, as set out in my *Identity and the Sacred* (1976) and the actual religious data in a variety of cultures. *The Fixed and the Fickle: Religion and Identity in New Zealand* (1981) was the first book in this research programme. The present study is the second. A third, on religion and identity in Canada, is in preparation.

The second purpose of this study is to assist some of the Australian economists of the Development Studies Centre of the Australian National University in their research on economic motivation and Aboriginal identity. Professor E. K. Fisk of the Centre played a large part in funding the project of which this book is the tangible result. I am very grateful for the gracious and generous manner in which he made the facilities of the Centre available. I hope that my social-scientific approach to the topic will be of some help in his search for an understanding of economic motivation and the breakdown of native integrity.

Others to whom this study owes much are three anthropologists, all far more knowledgeable in the field of Aboriginal religion than I ever could hope to be: Ronald Berndt, Kenelm Burridge, and William Stanner. Their writings and comments on the original draft were very useful. If their suggestions, together with the equally valuable ones of the readers selected by the Canadian Federation of the Humanities could not always be implemented, the reason lies in the physical impossibility of a return to the field in

Australia. Finally, I am very grateful that this book has been published with the help of a grant from the Canadian Federation for the Humanities, using funds provided by the Social Sciences and Humanities Research Council of Canada. Some of the material of chapters 1 and 2 has been used for my article "The Origin and Function of Religion: A Critique of, and Alternative to, Durkheim's Interpretation of the Religion of Australian Aborigines," *Journal for the Scientific Study of Religion*, 18/4 (December 1979), 379-89. I would like to thank the editor for permission to use the material.

January 1, 1982   Hans Mol

1

Religion and Identity

Religion preserves wholeness, regardless of whether a society is primitive or advanced. Or, to say this with the theme of this study, religion firms up or affirms what otherwise would be more formless and less whole.

What is it that otherwise "would be more formless"? In another work I have called it "identity" (Mol, 1976). There I contrasted identity (whether personal, group, tribal, social, or national) with change, or with those numerous elements (such as alienation, scepticism, culture contact, deviance, birth, death, marriage, divorce, conquests) which tend to weaken the boundaries around at least some of these identities. A conquering army breaks through the boundaries of a national identity. Similarly death or divorce may break down a family.

Identities always seem to have structure and delineated form. Yet they are usually precarious. Structure has to be defended in order to survive. If it is not, it will succumb in an inexorable jostle. Pacificism is not an option here. Yet the very jostling demands two paradoxical strategies: maintenance and change. A tribe will both defend its identity (and religion is one of the ways of doing this) and adapt, for instance, to a change in food supply.

Adaptation to an inhospitable environment means capacity both to counter change and to absorb it. Or to say this differently: it means to be capable of standing one's ground and to roll with the punches. In our context it means to defend the integrity of "forms" *and* to modify them.

In the intricate division of labour of even the most primitive society, such as an Australian aboriginal tribe, this two-pronged necessity is fully developed. For thousands of years native groups would not have survived in the desert unless everything had been geared to maximum knowledge and use of opportunities: the edibility of plants, the habits of animals, the storage of water. Yet opportunities can be chased so single-mindedly that they destroy the very context which makes them possible in the first place. Flexibility can dig its own grave. Formlessness can be as maladaptive as fixity. It is with this danger of identities and meanings becoming too ephemeral and formless that religions deal.

To understand the dialectic between the firm and the formless we must go back to primate history. Perhaps even further, for in a very general way the dialectic between structure and reaction in the inorganic world is balanced by a similar dialectic between heredity and variation in the organic one. And this biological interdependence is similar to the one between integration and differentiation in societies and cultures.

But to return to the more advanced life of the primates: territory is for them what identity is to humans. The wholeness or integrity of one's territory determines the maximization of opportunities and therefore survival. It is a relatively safe place to rear the young, and to assure oneself of food. It is easier to defend, because one knows all the nooks and crannies. An enemy which manages to penetrate to the heart of the territory will find a very determined animal as ardent in the defence of it as humans are in the defence of their family, their community, their country, or their personal integrity.

Yet certain animal species have gone further. They have survived because of concerted action. A school of small fishes or a flock of birds is a more formidable enemy for the shark or the hawk than the individual fish or bird. This means that sometimes conformity to the herd rather than maximization of individual aggression has proved to be the better solution of the survival problem. It also means that already in the animal world personal identity or individual integrity has become juxtaposed with group identity or social integrity. And in order to understand this juxtaposition well, these "wholes" or different levels of identity should be studied as *sui generis* phenomena. That is, the values (such as altruism) or rituals (such as mating dances) can only be understood incompletely if the individual or his gene is the only point of departure or the sole principle for understanding. Altruism can be understood much better if the social whole in which it functions is taken seriously as such.

The same applies to many of the animal rituals or ceremonies. They can be understood much more thoroughly if the pair, rather than the individual animal, is taken as the whole for which these rituals have reinforcing functions.

This does not mean that these various wholes do not have much in common. They do. They may differ on specific values, rituals, and so forth, but the need for maintaining or adapting and modifying any whole or identity is the same.

To return to human existence: here group or social wholeness has proved to have considerable evolutionary advantage. Human beings have always faced essentially the same problem as animals. To have the monopoly over a well-defined territory maximized the food supply. Yet this monopoly was only a ramshackle guarantee. Effective horde-cohesion furthered man's ecological niche, as it did and still does for many animal species. But man went further. The tribe with a co-ordinated division of labour in the defence or the attack would triumph. So, of course, would the tribe which made the best use of edible plants and developed weapons for the killing of animals. And symbols and language emerged to bolster the survival odds. A horde which possessed the means to communicate to its members how and where to approach the enemy, the predator, or the prey, or how and where to escape would have an advantage over other hordes where the aggressive instinct was not sufficiently disciplined for the common good.

All this means that very early in human existence horde-identity, as against personal identity, acquired its own separate and intricate rationale. This was true for many animals as well. Sociobiologists and anthropologists can profit equally from a rigorous application of the *ceteris paribus* principle in their respective fields. We can say the same differently: by constantly asking themselves the question, "Why did the horde which differed in one respect (such as capacity for sacrifice, or family attachment, or better communication, or a more elaborate ritual) survive over a horde where this one element was missing?" a better account of evolutionary development can be produced than when the reasoning is grounded on the survival of the individual within the species.

In human existence (in contrast with that of animals), sophisticated learning techniques have proved to be even better means than instinct, whether individual or social, for safeguarding the ecological niche.

But how does religion fit in? As soon as symbols and language emerge, knowledge beings to accumulate, values prove to be essential for cohesion, and the maintenance of order becomes more problematic. The problem is not just one of synchronic organization, but also of a diachronic order which spans the generations and is independent of birth and death. From the point of view of a viable social whole, the values and the meanings must be constantly reinforced. A reliable set of expectations must exist, if possible, for all eternity. Friction and tension must be minimized and solidarity maximized. Yet friction, tension, frustration, birth and death are inevitable. Identity is always precarious and is always in need of affirmation. The inevitabliity of change and disorder must therefore be made relative in terms of order. Their fateful consequences must be contained, not denied. Change and disorder are obvious enough. The destruction of form and structure is ubiquitous. Survival of identity therefore hinges on the fitting of chaos and disorder into a larger framework of order. This order is not just something to be believed in intellectually. Above all, it must be something to which the personnel of the whole of the tribe or the society is fully committed. It has to be anchored emotionally; it has to be ritually reinforced; it has to be reiterated in the tales and the myths.

Religion, then, is fundamentally linked with the problem of order in the various forms of identity of human existence. Many religions articulate this major concern by postulating the creation of order out of chaos. And chaos does not just consist of the unpredictability of earthquakes and floods, but also, and even primarily, of the unanticipated occurrences in human societies. An unexpected death disrupts as much as an immoral act. Chaos can be natural, social, and moral.

It is the chaotic possibility of life and the unpredictability of existence to which religion addresses itself. As said before: change is not denied, but contained, tamed, and relativized. Unless containment succeeds, the motivation of individuals to contribute to group or social wholeness may go by the board. Or, social or group identity may erode and be replaced by individual aggression and self-assertion. In such an instance motivation becomes based on advantage for the individual rather than the common good. The common good must be represented in a viable, legitimated whole, if it is to have an effect on individual action. Lack of motivation is therefore one of the first and major symptoms of a sick society or group within that society. Deviance, alcoholism, delinquency, corruption are all symptoms of social inability to motivate individuals to promote the common good. Alienated people or groups are a threat to a particular social order. Depending on the cohesion of that society, measures will be taken to restore the balance.

Yet sometimes the amount of change has been so great that the normal mechanisms for restoring identity are insufficient. Stone-age people confronted with Western technology do not have the resources (social, religious, or military) to rescue their integrity. The first symptoms of collapse consist in the alienation, purposelessness, and lack of motivation of the tribal membership. An intricate system of social rewards and punishments has become irrelevant and no amount of Western provisions can restore the balance.

Particularly in the case of Australian Aboriginals the gap between stone-age and Western culture has proved to be so great that the motivation of individuals has suffered severely. In chapters two to five of this study we will trace the intricate relation between identity and religion in traditional Aboriginal society. In chapters six and seven we will attempt to investigate in which ways religion either has been able to restore the old identity in part or has helped in the formation of a new one.

However, before doing so, it may be useful to recapitulate here the four mechanisms which religion provides for the sacralization of identity. Sacralization is the process by means of which man has pre-eminently safeguarded and reinforced this complex of orderly interpretations of reality, rules, and legitimations. The mechanisms of sacralization can be broken down into at least the following categories:

1. objectification (the projection of order into a beyond where it is less vulnerable to contradictions, exceptions, and contingencies—in other words a rarefied realm where major outlines of order can be maintained in the face of temporal, but all-absorbing dislocations of that order);

2. commitment (the emotional anchorage in the various, proliferating foci of identity);

3. ritual (the repetitive actions, articulations, and movements which prevent the object of sacralization from being lost sight of);

4. myth (the integration of the various strains in a coherent, shorthand, symbolic account).

1. Identity in Aboriginal Society

Clan- or horde-identity is fundamental in Aboriginal society. It is basic both in the sense of social organization (the cohesion is very strong) and in the sense of an exclusive link with a particular territory. The clan, and beyond it, the tribe, has a clearly defined place in the environment. Yet this place is always precarious. Scarcities of one sort or another could, and did, easily lead to starvation and famine. Clans are therefore closely bound together by common suffering, but also by common joy and achievement, by common rules and patterns of socialization.

The clans, as Ronald Berndt (1976, 133) has it, "built up protective crusts or sociocultural buffers which define their place in nature while at the same time bringing nature into a familiar and manageable frame of reference." Adaptation required that the environment would have to be continually wrapped up "into a meaningful package."

Group identity is anchored in the land. It is the land which is peopled by the ancestors, and therefore the ties between clan and country are unbreakable. Munn (1970, 143) quotes a Pitjantjatjara (Central Australia) woman as saying that her various body markings, such as moles, warts, or skin discolorations, were the same marks as those left by the ancestors upon a particular ancestral rock at her birthplace. Identity, countryside, and ancestry are interwoven into one stable structure. The country is "a network of places joined by various ancestral routes." And this "world of forms (a visually defined, named and socially segmented order), laid down by ancestral beings, mediates the relationships between the untrammelled creativity of ancestors and the dependent receptivity of living human beings . . . ." (ibid., 148). The delineations of the land and social organization are secure forms of order. Formlessness is disorder. Classification is order. An identity which is not clearly defined is incomplete and therefore dangerous. It is as dangerous as the unknown lands, the unknown people, and the unknown tongues beyond the familiar forms and boundaries. Therefore, native guides are often loath to go beyond their tribal borders. Forays into other areas are not often successful. The natives lose heart in the "country of unknown totemic heroes and spirit-centres some of which might be lethal to those who did not know how to approach them" (Elkin, 1974, 69). Loss of identity and paralysis of motivation go hand in hand. Or as Spencer and Gillen (1904, 31-32) have expressed it: "Anything strange is uncanny to the native, who has a peculiar dread of evil magic from a distance. Our two 'boys' who went with us right through the continent were particularly careful to keep close to camp, unless well-armed, when they got amongst absolutely strange tribes in the country out to the east of the telegraph line."

The clan was by no means the only meaningful identity in traditional Aboriginal society. Moieties (usually the exogamous half of a tribe), tribes (consisting of many clans), maleness (or femaleness) were all significant social units. So was the individual, however much he was supposed to conform to the intricate set of rules and expectations. Although his subordination was shown in the rare use of his personal name (Burridge, 1973, 136), his personhood was guaranteed through his unique link with a specific ancestral spirit which had entered his mother's womb at the time of conception. In the Murimbata tribe (South-West Arnhem Land) each person had his or her private totem (*Mir*) which could consist of "virtually any entity in the universe—fire, lightning, smoke, the sea, sickness" (Stanner, 1966, 32), but was always associated with a notable incident at his or her conception.

However, the *Mir* already leads us into the discussion of the sacralization of a specific (personal) identity and it may be better to do this more systematically under a different heading.

2

Objectification

Central to the idea of objectification as used here is the word "order." Identities of one sort or another are strengthened when they are linked to an order which sums up what the identity in question is all about. The order is all the more effective when a united consensus and commitment exist about that order. The element of commitment will be discussed in the next section. Here the accent lies on the objectifying process rather than on the attachment to the objectified point of reference.

It is the objectifying process which we also want to separate from our fourth mechanism, myth and belief. There the emphasis is on the content of the objectified point of reference. Here we have a more historical, evolutionary purpose in mind: we want to pay special attention to the increasing abstraction of the objectified point of reference as a means for straddling an increasingly complex society, and we want to stress the order provision relevant for a concrete society.

There is ample evidence that commitment, ritual, and myth are very much part of all societies. Therefore a synchronic or a-historical account is sufficient. Based on observations of advanced societies it is not too difficult to see very similar mechanisms operating in other societies. But this is not true for the objectifying process. Here there is a progression to increasing abstraction and therefore a diachronic or historical account should generally be incorporated. After all, history is important and a prerequisite for the understanding of ourselves and the evolutionary context of our existence.

Aboriginal society is such an interesting phenomenon because its objectified, or order-providing, point of reference is both concrete and multiple. It is concrete in that it deals with the animate or inanimate objects of the environment. It is multiple in that the significant "wholenesses" or identities of Aboriginal existence are all neatly provided with their own objectified point of reference. We have in mind the system of totems or totemism.

1. Totemism

A totem in Aboriginal society is always a tangible or visible object. It may be an animal, a plant, a rock, a rainbow, or even "cold weather." More important than its physical appearance is what it represents. Some scholars think of it as an emblem of a tribe, a clan, females or males, a person, or a moiety (often the exogamous half of a tribe): all the major and most significant identities of Aboriginal society. The "emblem" is treated with special respect. Certainly the original meaning of totem (it is an Algonquin Canadian Indian word) was emblem or badge.

Actually it is more than an emblem, because Aboriginals claim that they descend from their totem. It also represents a partly human, partly animal ancestor. As such it is more than the rainbow totem so well described by Ralph Linton (1924) as the emblem of the 42nd Division of the American Expeditionary Force during World War I. Linton describes how the rainbow became the cohesive rallying point for the unit to which he belonged.

Early European observers of totemism (which in our terms is a system of meaning in which environmental objects are reverently linked to a variety of identities) tended to look down upon what they thought to be a rather childish, inferior, primitive form of religion. Only an untutored, irrational mind, so they thought, could make a lowly animal the revered ancestor of man.

In terms of our perspective on religion, totemism is an astute delineation of the major identities of Aboriginal existence. And as such it differs not that much from other delineations of order, such as the ones to which scientists are committed or the one Linton describes. The major difference, as we have said before, is the degree of abstraction of Western man's ever-widening conceptual universe. Yet there is similarity in basic commitments to order and delineations of that order.

By contrast, Aboriginal totemism is very concrete. Nature as a straddling concept does not exist. The Australian natives may think about a clan or a person as a whole, or as a wallaby, or a bandicoot, but nature is only dealt with in the variety of its aspects. They are too close to nature to distance themselves from it. It is for this reason that totemism differs considerably from nature religion (Elkin, 1974, 166).

Australian totemism has received a great deal of attention from anthropologists and sociologists alike. By discussing their theories, we may learn how far their views fit with our "identity" perspective.

2.   Sir James Frazer

Sir James Frazer was not the first to take an active interest in totemism. However, he wrote four massive volumes on the subject and they exerted considerable influence. He was also very much a child of his age. Totemism was therefore seen through the eyes of someone who took rational individualism as the only valid key of interpretation and assumed it to be the goal of evolution.

With respect to individualism, totemism, he said, is designed to meet the need of the ordinary individual (Frazer, 1910, Vol. 1, 117). The conception totem (the totem belonging to the place where the individual for the first time made his presence known in the womb), not the social or group totems, was the foundation and origin of totemism. "Conceptual totemism pure and simple furnishes an intelligible starting-point for the evolution of totemism in general" (Vol. 1, 161).

With respect to rationalism, Frazer saw Australian totemism as fundamentally the magic of "the most backward of mankind." The proof lay in the fact that the most important and striking native ceremonies were an attempt to "compel nature to do their bidding and so to supply all their wants" (1937, 257). Or, as he had said much earlier (1910, Vol. 4, 61), "The ultimate source of totemism is a savage ignorance of the physical process by which men and animals reproduce their kinds."

Both assumptions are wrong. Australian totems are not fundamentally concerned with subsistence, but with the delineation of a variety of intricately interwoven wholes: tribes, moieties, clans, sexes, individuals. These intertwining identities showed considerable social organization and emerged initially probably because each of them assisted the survival of tribes over those which did not have them. Neither are totems the best available means for the rational explanation and manipulation of the environment. Rational explanation is a far less critical issue than Frazer and many others assumed. More important was the anchoring of the delineations in the emotions through reverence or rituals.

3. Emile Durkheim

Durkheim was a decided advance over Frazer in that he challenged the rational individualism of the age. Yet in doing so he made the opposite mistake. Not the individual, but the social, not the rational, but the "collective effervescence," lay at the root of totemism, he said. Totemism to Durkheim was the most elementary form of religion. And behind it, in turn, lay the deepest universal principle, its social function. "The totem is the source of the moral life of the clan" (1965, 219). Moreover, he said, all religions have their ultimate source in this social function. Society is to its members "what a god is to his worshippers . . . a being whom men think of as superior to themselves" (ibid., 237).

Durkheim did not see any discrepancy between this discovery and the existence of totems which tended to divide rather than unite a society. Sexual totemism (a special totem, such as the emu for the males and the woodpecker for the females) represented the separate conditions in which the sexes lived (ibid., 193), but he assumed that they could be harmoniously related to clan totems. Similarly with individual totems. They were less relevant because, in contrast with class totems, the individual never claimed descent from this personal protector, friend, and associate (ibid., 188). In addition a personal totem is frequently optional (ibid., 191), a convenience rather than a necessity. It is an outside projection, power, judge, and helper (ibid., 317). Again, the separateness and distinctiveness of the individual totem as compared with the clan totem does not worry Durkheim. After all, the conception totem is a uniquely individual totem in which ancestral descent is a central feature. It is determined by the locality where the ancestral spirit entered the body of the mother. Or, as Falkenberg (1962, 238) puts it, individuality is recognized "by the fact that each person possesses from birth to death, an individual totem and individual names."

As stated above Durkheim made the opposite mistake to Frazer. He was so intent upon disproving the prevailing theories which explain "the complex by the simple, the totem of the group by that of the individual" (1965, 200), that he made the individual secondary to the social. Or, as he said quite plainly, "the individual soul is only a portion of the collective soul of the group" (ibid., 299). "If the soul is a part of the divine substance, it represents something not ourselves that is within us. . . . Society [is the] unique source of all that is sacred" (ibid., 297). It did not occur to Durkheim that the soul could be the objectification of personal identity as separate and distinct from objectification of group and social identity.

Neither Durkheim's nor Frazer's view is correct. The relation between individual and group is dialectic rather than subsidiary. But for a more dialectical appreciation of totemism we have to wait for the later Radcliffe-Brown and for Lévi-Strauss. Here it suffices to use as an example of the conflict between individual and clan totem the case of Albert Namatjira's father in Central Australia. He eloped with a girl from the "wrong" kin-group class. Not only did the father have to take severe corporeal punishment (spearing of the thigh) for the deviant act, but he was also excluded from instruction by his elders into the sacred traditions of his own conception site, the flying-ant totemic centre of Intalua (Strehlow, 1970, 122).

4. Sigmund Freud

Although Freud wrote *Totem and Taboo* shortly after Durkheim's *Elementary Forms of the Religious Life*, his analysis of totemism was basically a regression to Frazer. He, like Frazer, overemphasized the significance of totemism for the person at the expense of social cohesion. And although Freud was singularly aware of the place of sentiment, his own explanatory principle was strongly informed by rational individualism as the acme of creation.

To Freud totemism had its roots in the Oedipus complex. "The totem," he said (1946, 5), "is first of all the tribal ancestor of the clan." Therefore the clan members cannot kill or eat the totem. Also, "members of the same totem are not allowed to enter into sexual relations with each other; that is that they cannot marry each other" (ibid., 7). To Freud this meant the universal incest taboo. He was aware of sex and individual totems (which do not fit his explanation), but he says (ibid., 134), these totems "are comparatively of little importance and . . . recent formations." And as for the conception totems, they are "a creation of the feminine mind and . . . sick fantasies of the pregnant woman" (ibid., 153).

Freud is aware of Frazer's correct observation that "totemism and exogamy are fundamentally distinct" (ibid., 155), but sexuality was his ordering principle and so this observation had to be rejected.

Freud's psychoanalytical solution was that "the totem animal is really a substitute for the father . . . the envied and feared model for each of the brothers" (ibid., 182-83), who obstructs their wish to marry the mother. The totem feast is the commemoration of their devouring him and acquiring part of his strength. Yet the remorse for this proto-historical act issues in the general prohibition of eating the father substitute and of sexual intercourse with the liberated women (ibid., 185).

Freud's account contains some errors of fact. For instance, clans and moieties may be exogamous, but tribes, sexes, and individuals are obviously not. His account is memorable as an illustration of the totemic principle. There is the same reverence and commitment to a particular principle delineating and summarizing order: "totem" in the case of Australian aborigines and "sexuality" in the case of Freud.

The differences are threefold:

1. Facts and interpretations dovetailed better in the Aboriginal context.

2. Abstract justifications were non-existent in traditional Aboriginal society.

3. In contrast with the actual totems of Aboriginal society, rational individualism was to Freud the most important latent principle of interpretation. Sexuality was the most important overt or manifest one. As a result Freud mistakenly disallowed the link between incest taboo and inbreeding. His grounds were that psychoanalysis had observed that "the first sexual impulses of the young are regularly of an incestuous nature" (ibid., 160). As Freud bases his argument on the fact of exogamy, it would have been more pertinent if he had asked himself why exogamous clans survived over endogamous ones. The question would have inevitably directed the attention to social norms rather than individual propensities.

5. A. R. Radcliffe-Brown

Radcliffe-Brown was another famous scholar who looked at Aboriginal totems with coloured glasses. For him the unifying principle summing up his understanding of life did not consist of rational individualism, as with Frazer, or social solidarity, as with Durkheim, or sexuality, as with Freud. It was much more simple. It was food. Like solidarity and sexuality, food, too, is a prerequisite for survival and as such cannot be too far from an explanatory key.

What was Radcliffe-Brown's argument? The very diverse forms of totemism must have had very diverse origins (1961, 122). Yet these may be successive modifications from a single form. Durkheim satisfactorily explained some form of totemism, but the explanation is incomplete. Totemism also has non-social functions (ibid., 125). Nor did Durkheim have a good explanation for the fact that the emblems were so often animals or plants. Further, Durkheim's theory fails to denote the larger class of ritual relations between man and the natural species, of which totemism is only a subclass. This larger class includes "the ritual attitude of the Andaman Islanders towards the turtle, of Californian Indians to the salmon, of the peoples of North America and Northern Asia to the bear" (ibid., 126). "Natural species are selected as representatives of social groups, such as clans, because they are already objects of the ritual attitude on quite another basis . . ." (129). That basis may be found in the increase ceremonies (rituals in which the increase of the totemic animals is sought), which Radcliffe-Brown regards as "a sort of co-operative effort, involving a division of [ritual] labour, by which the normal processes of nature and the supply of food are provided for" (ibid).

Twenty years later Radcliffe-Brown provided a somewhat different and more sophisticated slant on totemism. Again he asked the questions, Why are Aboriginal social groups associated with a particular natural species? What is the principle behind the choice of such pairs as eagle-hawk and crow, the wombat and the kangaroo, the white cockatoo and crow, representing moieties or alternating generation divisions (grandparents and grandsons versus fathers and their son's children)? (1958, 108-12).

The answer: in all Australian tales of this kind the pairs represent opponents in some sort of conflict. Thinking in terms of opposites, upwards and downwards, strong and weak, black and white are universal features of human thinking. There is a general law that in the case of exogamous moieties the latter are regarded in opposing terms—black versus white cockatoos, for instance (ibid., 118). Teasing relationships, competitive games, Oxford and Cambridge are in the same category (ibid., 120). This uniting (cockatoo) and separating (black and white), this union of opposites or unity of contraries is similar to *Yin* (the feminine) and *Yang* (the masculine) united in *Tao* (order) in ancient China (ibid., 124).

Radcliffe-Brown provides another interesting example of totems used in conflict. In New South Wales tension between the sexes of a particular clan is expressed by killing a bat (the "brother" or sex totem of the men) and leaving it lying in the camp for the men to see (ibid., 125). The men retaliate by killing the bird, which is the sex totem of the women. After a fight, the air is then cleared and peace restored. Radcliffe-Brown (ibid., 116) guesses that the differences and similiarities between bat and bird are a totemic dramatization of conflict and friendship, opposition and solidarity, in human society.

This theme is reminiscent of Arnold van Gennep (1920, 351) who, more than three decades earlier, in the last sentence of his discussion of the forty-one theories of totemism, stressed its function to unite what of necessity is divided (e.g., locality and parentage) and thereby to promote cohesion.

Radcliffe-Brown's and van Gennep's accounts of totemism are important advances over Durkheim in that they make room for the very totems which divide. Yet the problem with Radcliffe-Brown's later interpretation of totemism is its restricted explanatory power. After all, many totems do *not* have counterparts, are *not* animals or plants. Obviously we need a better theory than either Frazer, Durkheim, Freud, or Radcliffe-Brown provides.

Understandably the next major anthropologist to be considered, Lévi-Strauss, leans strongly on Radcliffe-Brown's union of opposites, but unfortunately falls equally (if not further) short of the goal of providing a universal frame of reference.

6. Claude Lévi-Strauss

Another major scholar who has given careful thought to Australian totemism is Lévi-Strauss. To him the key to understanding lay in yet a different category. Accepting the fact that totems do not fall into a recognizable class (features of nature, animals, plants, and so forth), he points out that it is precisely the difference between the totems which is crucial. They designate differences in social relationships. Totemic thinking is a way of thinking characteristic of our own society. The key to totemism is therefore not "rational individualism," "social solidarity," "sexuality," "food," but "cognition."

Lévi Strauss (with a bow to the American distaste for anything totemic) begins by dismantling or relativizing all previous theories of totemism as "illusions." He is not interested in the unique content of totemism or what it is trying to explain. To attempt this, he says, leads nowhere, or to an illusory conceptual coherence (1963, 18). He is more interested in relations between the significant terms, such as sex and social totems. Although he acknowledges his debt to great ethnographers, such as Elkin, he refuses to follow the latter when he takes totems as a *sui generis* reality (ibid., 46). One can drive a carriage, he says, between Elkin's penetrating enquiries and summary synthesis (ibid., 55).

He is not much kinder to the functionalists, such as Malinowski, Firth, Freud, and Durkheim, whom he correctly accuses of always thinking in terms of causes and effects rather than in terms of binary oppositions. The "natural species are chosen not because they are 'good to eat' [the earlier Radcliffe-Brown and Malinowski] but because they are 'good to think'" (ibid., 89). As for Durkheim, while he may be right in saying that there is something arbitrary about the totem as such (later, Stanner, 1965, 227, would similarly suggest that they probably were "irreducibly arbitrary"), he like Freud, is definitely wrong in giving priority to sentiments and emotions (Lévi-Strauss, 1963, 70). After all, "it is not present emotions, felt at gatherings and ceremonies, which engender or perpetuate the rites, but ritual activity which arouses the emotions. . . . Actually impulses and emotions explain nothing: they are always results, either of the power of the body or of the impotence of the mind. In both cases they are consequences, never causes" (ibid., 71).

It is not accidental that this cognitive overbalancing by Lévi-Strauss in opposition to Durkheim is rather analogous to a similar social overbalancing by Durkheim in opposition to Frazer.

Lévi-Strauss (ibid., 94) has more appreciation for Bergson's observation that totemism allows for distinctions between clans. Yet he correctly takes issue with Bergson when the latter stresses exogamy as an instinct preventing biologically harmful unions between close relatives. "But," bristles Lévi-Strauss, "if such an instinct existed, a recourse to institutions would be superfluous" (ibid.).

Lévi-Strauss is both excitingly progressive and regrettably regressive. His approach is progressive in that the dialectical method, or the stress on the reconciliation of binary oppositions, allows for a roomier, more universal accounting scheme than the mono-causal, often culture-bound theorizing of Frazer, Durkheim, Freud, and the early Radcliffe-Brown. The latent sense of Western superiority over savage habits has been demolished by Lévi-Strauss. The fruitless search for the totemic explanation in terms of physical characteristics or of incest taboo has been turned into a more fruitful quest for the totemic delineation and resolution of oppositions.

And yet the approach is also regressive in that ultimately Lévi-Strauss falls into the same trap into which Frazer fell: the overestimation of individual rationalism. His own totemic ordering, the principle of cognition, prevents him from adopting a roomier accounting scheme, in which the rational, analytical mode is in dialectic with the emotive, synthetic, integrative mode. Or to say this in our terminology: identity is secondary to rationality and differentiation, rather than its integrative counterpart. And this means a fundamental distortion of religion. Religion restores the integrative counterbalance, as Durkheim saw dimly. (Dimly, because Durkheim thought in terms of integration, but not in terms of counterbalance.) In addition, Lévi-Strauss is insensitive to the reinforcing effect which the totem has on various identities. He is too interested in structure to have much eye for the function and content of separate wholes.

Taking cognition as his ordering principle, Lévi-Strauss, almost by definition (definitions confine!), has to play down the very elements which reinforce the cognitive delineations: emotional attachments. Nature is to culture as the affective life is to intellectuality, as he approvingly found in Rousseau (1963, 100). Yet it is this entire area of emotional detachments from, and attachments to, a large variety of identities which is crucial for the understanding of such diverse phenomena as charismatic movements, religious conversions, and rites of passage. Yet there is no place for them in the Lévi-Straussian scheme.

7. William E. H. Stanner

A very astute observer and interpreter of Australian totemism is William Stanner. He sums totemism up as a principle of order transcending everything significant for Aboriginal man (1972, 270) or as the listing or mapping of a family of sets (1965, 225). Regarding the totems of the Murimbata (a tribe in South-West Arnhem Land with which he lived), he says that they stood for the identity of, and unity between, persons known to possess them (1966, 152). Elsewhere he calls totemism "the language of the ontological system" (ibid., 35). Its function is to mediate the first-ordained order (ibid., 31).

This objectified, ordained order (or fixation or instituting of things in an enduring form, as he terms it elsewhere; 1965, 214) is called "The Dreaming." It is a word which the Aboriginals themselves use when they want to translate for English-speaking people what the *alcheringa* (the Aranda word) or *tjukurpa* (the Pitjandara word) is all about. It can also mean "ancestry," as with the Walbiri, for whom the "basic term for 'dream,' *djugurba*, also denotes the period of time when the ancestors lived. . . . The ancestors themselves are also called *djugurba*" (Munn, 1964, 81).

In fact the word is untranslatable, as it combines many elements which the Western mind strictly separates: reality, symbol, body, spirit, totem, spirit-site. The Dreaming is a "unity of waking-life and dream-life" (Stanner, 1972, 271). It is so close to the native that he thinks of the person and the totem as one. Nature in the abstract does not exist for him. Nor do time and history. Or to say this in our own terms: marginality or alienation are impossibilities for the traditional aboriginal. They are worse than death. Detachment is beyond question, because the founding drama of The Dreaming is in the self, the clan, the totem, the physical surroundings—all indissolubly one.

We will return to Stanner's observation in the chapters on ritual and myth. Totemism can be summed up as an embryonic objectification. It represents an order in terms of which existence is interpreted. However much the individual, clan, or tribe is part and parcel of that order, The Dreaming is also an interpreter or reconciler for the individual, clan, or tribe, rather analogous to the actual function of an actual dream for the individual (Mol, 1976, 258ff). It is this embryonic quality of the objectification mechanism which makes one sympathetic to the much reviled statement by Durkheim (1965, 13-15) that Aboriginal religion represented the most primitive and simplest of religions. That may not be true for our other sacralization mechanisms (commitment, ritual, and myth), but there is no denying that totemism represents a transcendental order with very little transcendence. One can indeed construct a continuum from an embryonic objectification to one impossibly far removed (e.g., Nirwana). Similarly one can observe that with progressively greater transcendentalization or abstract objectification the advanced religions played with fire. After all, marginality is the enemy of all religion. It is marginality which puts identity and motivation in jeopardy. And yet Western civilization has successfully played with that fire. Without the detachment from existing structure, without condoning marginality, nature could not have been manipulated and mastered. The great difficulties which Australian Aboriginals have encountered in coming to terms with Western civilization are likely related to the considerable distance between embryonic and full-fledged objectification. One's view of order is intimately connected with the range of actions one considers viable. And motivation is only another word for action considered both plausible and desirable.

8.   Other Forms of Objectification

It has been our assumption that in more complex societies the objectified frame of reference has to become more general in order to straddle meaningfully a variety of specific identities. Instead of a special totem (concrete in itself) for a concrete unit of organization, a more general, more abstract order emerges to interpret and reinforce the mundane delineations.

Some of the earlier scholars who studied Australian Aboriginal society detected the beginnings of a belief system of high gods or sky-beings. Particularly in Eastern Australia there existed a rather widespread system of beliefs and myths about sky-beings. They were thought to be responsible for showing the tribes their respective territories, for creating the landscape, for providing men with implements, rules, and, above all, initiation rites. Their names were secret. So secret, in fact, that in some instances the name was lost to posterity when only women and uninitiated males remained of a dying race. Only initiates would learn of the belief at the final and most solemn phase of the initiation rites. These sky-beings were all-seeing and all-knowing. They had a rather close relation with the medicine-men who would visit them on nocturnal flights (Elkin, 1974, 252-53).

The surviving names of these spirit-beings differed from one region to another. The tribes in Northern New South Wales called him Baiame. He was to them the final and unimpeachable authority for customs and sanctions, in much the same way as The Dreaming was in Central and North-Western Australia (ibid., 254).

Bunjil was the sky-being for the Kulin nation and the Wot-jobaluk in Western Victoria. Bunjil meant eagle-hawk (Howitt, 1904, 126) and was considered an old, benign father of all the people, who had two wives and a son by the name of Binbeal, who was the rainbow. He lived on earth but moved to the sky in a whirlwind where he has been ever since, watching the Kulin (ibid., 492).

Howitt, interestingly, notes the preponderance of the human over the animal element in Bunjil. "In fact, I cannot see any trace of the latter in him" (ibid., 492). He was the creator of the earth, trees, and men, and his name stood for wisdom or knowledge. Before he went to live in the sky, Bunjil taught men the use of nets, canoes, and weapons. This emerging differentiation between the human and the environment and the objectification of order in the human alone is also typical of sky-beings in other districts of South-East Australia.

There were substantial differences between them, though. The sky-being of the Kurnai (in South-East Victoria), so the story goes, was less benign and became very angry indeed when some secrets were divulged to women. He sent his fire, the Aurora Australis, to earth and in the subsequent holocaust "men went mad with fear, and speared each other, fathers killing their children, husbands their wives, and brethren each other" (ibid., 493). The sea did the rest and almost all those who had managed to survive the slaughter were drowned.

Daramulun was the sky-being of the Yuin in the South-East of New South Wales. He and his mother were the first inhabitants of the earth, which extended "far out where the sea is now" at the time when there were "no men and women and only animals, birds and reptiles." Daramulun planted trees and after a flood went "to the sky where he lives and watches the actions of men." He gives the Yuins their laws and their magic and is very angry when they eat forbidden food. He also takes care of the deceased (ibid., 495).

Nurrendere and Martummere are the names given to the sky-being of the Narrinyeri, a tribe on the southern side of the St. Vincent Gulf in South Australia. He is the creator of all things existing, the giver of weapons, and the institutor of rites and ceremonies.

There has been a long-standing controversy about the authenticity of the sky-beings (Stanner's name), sky-heroes (Elkin's term), or high gods (Eliade's word). Were they Aboriginal adaptations from missionary sermons, as Tylor suggested, or native inventions to satisfy European curiosity, as Baldwin Spencer thought (Eliade, 1973, 10)? The evolutionists, such as Spencer, Frazer, and Hartland, were convinced that high gods and totems could not possibly exist together, as they belonged to quite different stages of evolutionary development. On the other hand, Andrew Lang and Wilhelm Schmidt maintained that they were reconcilable, as the idea of a god in heaven could very well precede totemic ideas or primitive myths.

None of present-day Australian anthropologists is very interested in this controversy, which raged in the first half of this century. But in his recent book on Australian religions Eliade (1973) has revived it at the expense of totemism, mainly because historians of religion regard it as a vital issue. Whatever the merits of the case, there is very strong evidence of sky-beings and totemic heroes existing happily together in traditional Aboriginal society (Elkin, 1974, 253).

After a detailed summary of the controversy, Eliade solves the problem to his own satisfaction by saying that the "religious function of the primordial and primordiality remains the same" (1973, 40), which I take to mean that both totems and high gods fulfilled the same purpose. The problem with Eliade's solution is that his "primordiality" means "primordial mythical time" or the *illud tempus* when all that was "real, meaningful, exemplary, and of inexhaustible creativity" (ibid.) was formed and effected.

The problem is that time in that sense is foreign to totemism. To Aborigines time is not "a horizontal line extending back chronologically through a series of pasts but rather a vertical line in which the past underlies and is within the present" (Elkin, 1969, 93). It makes more sense to think in terms of an objectified order (whether peopled with ancestral totems or high gods, or both) which contained, tamed, and relativized the mundane with its potential for disorder. If high gods fitted better in more complex societies, that does not therefore make them irrelevant for Aboriginal society, as the over-rigid evolutionists appear to assume.

More important, the distinction between totemic ancestors and high gods is overdone. Are the stars and the sky or the angry sky-being with his wives and children so much more "spiritual" than the ant-hill and the bandicoot? If there is any distinction, I would rather opt for Howitt's observation of an increasing differentiation between man and his environment. Of greater importance, too, is the limited relevance of high gods for objectifying clan or tribal orders when they were so obviously confined to initiation secrets.

Still, the issue needs to be thought through more carefully, if only because its solution would be relevant for comparative religion. A very similar debate is going on about the authenticity of a system of high gods in traditional Maori society. Was the cult of Io a local New Zealand development confined to the *tohunga* training centres, called *Whare Wananga*? Or was it a later addition to counter the competition of the missionaries? That issue also remains unresolved (Mol, 1982).

Whatever the specific character of specific objectifications, to us the existence and functioning of a supramundane order as such is significant enough. Just as important is the emotional attachment and commitment to a transcendental frame of reference, however embryonic the transcendence happens to be. It is to this topic that we now turn.

3

Commitment

Commitment to order is a prerequisite for the survival of the latter. Therefore societies instill loyalty in their constituencies. The delineations of order are impotent, unless they are anchored in the emotions. Here we will summarize the part played by commitments, sentiments, and emotions for the maintenance of boundaries in traditional Aboriginal society. A commitment is an antidote to the formless. It affirms order.

1. Taboos

Taboos maintain and deepen the grooves around identities. They strengthen the "within" and separate it from the "without." Feelings of dread and awe hedge and articulate the classifications.

Totems illustrate this general rule. It is generally forbidden to eat the totem animal or plant. Every time a member of the lizard clan encounters a lizard, he is reminded of both its and the clan's separateness. It has been set aside. If it is to be eaten at all (in modest amounts), it is done at solemn occasions, such as clan ceremonies.

This injunction can lead to problems. Spencer and Gillen (1904, 160) mention the awkwardness experienced by members of the water clan who, if men from other clans are present, can only receive water through them. In this instance as well as others the taboo unites the members of the one and separates them from other clans. The prohibitions remind them constantly of who they are.

In the same way as sacrifice clarifies a system of priorities (Mol, 1976, 226), so the taboo clarifies the priority of the clan collectivity over a specific need for food or water. Of course the reminder can take other forms, such as the anthill, or lightning. Yet when the taboo consists of something edible or potable, the refraining as such has an additional delineating force.

Food taboos emotionally anchor other divisions as well, such as those between age- and sex-groups. In certain tribes the prohibition of certain desirable foods is relaxed according to age. In this way the age hierarchy is reinforced and old age becomes a desirable status.

Food taboos figure largely in the initiation ceremonies of the Narrinyeri (southern area of South Australia). Youths about to be initiated are forbidden to eat any food belonging to women, and the other way around: any animal or fish caught by the youths is forbidden to all females. Women cannot eat food procured by others with the implements of the initiates (Howitt, 1904, 674-75). It is as though food here is the vehicle for accentuating the division between the young men and their mothers or other females to whom they were attached sentimentally as children.

Aboriginal society has numerous marriage taboos. A man and a woman can only marry outside well-defined clan and kinship classes. Feelings can run very high when a couple thwarts these rules, so much so that killer parties have been known to hunt down the eloping pair of incompatible kinship classes.

Another interesting and widespread taboo exists about relations with one's mother-in-law. The son-in-law is not allowed to use his wife's mother's name and must avoid face-to-face contact with her. This means that if they camp together they must be segregated in different areas. Or they must change direction if they happen to walk toward each other. Elkin (1974, 149) suggests that this taboo is a way of avoiding "any competition between a girl and her mother for the affections of the same man—a danger which might be very real where so often the husband and mother-in-law are of the same age." On the other hand, the taboo could be a way to delineate the family in which one grew up from the family established through marriage. This interpretation gains even more credibility when it is remembered that the avoidance is often extended to father- and brother-in-law. One may even defend the view that this particular kind of taboo is a rather effective reminder of the separation and reconstitution of families, comparable to the Western, "once-and-for-all," wedding rites of passage.

There are other taboos, for instance, the death-site taboo. As soon as death occurs, the clan moves camp. Here too the taboo may delineate the clan's previous existence from the new one, excluding the recently departed. It is as though the mobility (not too difficult to achieve anyway amongst nomads) erases one delineation to make room for another. Death rites, of course do the same and we will return to this topic in the chapter on ritual.

2. Leadership

Sentiments of solidarity are often projected on leadership figures. Ruling hierarchies are treated with awe as representing the unity of empire, tribe, or country. Yet Aboriginal society is singularly devoid of this kind of leadership. There is no trace of the sacralization of hierarchies as, for instance, in Maori society (Mol, 1981). Particularly, the general absence of anything resembling charismatic leadership may be one of the many reasons why aborigines have usually failed to establish a new identity after the erosion of the old one. It is charismatic leadership which on the social level can be rather effective in stripping away an old identity and welding a new one (Mol, 1976, 45).

In Aboriginal society leadership and authority are not carried out very decisively. Yet there are gradations of power within the clans. The older men are more powerful than the younger ones, and these in turn are more powerful than the women. Ritual leaders generally wield important authority, and one might expect this to shade over into the secular realm. Yet Warner (1964, 379) notes that the power of a ritual leader is at "an absolute minimum" in other realms. "The idea of a formal chief, or a leader with authority, just does not seem to make sense to a blackfellow" (Stanner, 1972, 277). Strehlow (1970, 106) observes almost everywhere in Central Australia "an absence of effective secular leadership." The same author (123) gives the example of bone-pointing at an arrogant leader, who subsequently died.

Jack McLaren, in his book *My Crowded Solitude* (1926, 144), tells the amusing story of his utter inability to find a native overseer for his coconut plantation on the York peninsula. His choicest workers would readily enough accept the additional tobacco, flour, and tinned food which went with the job, but would utterly fail in exercising any discipline over the tribal workforce. Who were they to rebuke the labourers when they came and left when they pleased and slept away whole afternoons? They were their own people, their brothers, their friends. The supposed overseers could not speak harshly to them, for they would regard them as hard and cruel and dislike them.

Yet law and order were maintained, generally by means of consensus of the older men. Once a decision was reached, offenders would be executed for a serious crime without further ado. Sometimes not even consensus was required for an execution. It was taken for granted that women or children who either accidentally or purposely watched the secret male ceremonies from which they were expressly excluded would be speared forthwith.

The position of ritual leader and medicine-man in Aboriginal society was quite powerful (as it still is in Arnhem Land, for instance). He can cure the sick and be the go-between of the people and The Dreaming. In South-Western Victoria the medicine-man was thought to go up into the clouds to bring down a spirit with whom he could inspect the body of the patient (Elkin, 1977, 75). He is also a clairvoyant who can see into the future. He presides at inquests when sorcery is thought to be the cause of death. At such an occasion his expert knowledge of personal relations within the tribe is crucial.

Both Elkin (ibid., 17ff.) and Eliade (1973, 131ff.) elaborate on the initiation of the medicine-man. Prominent again is the rebirth theme: in some regions he is ritually swallowed by a snake in a waterhole and later ejected as a newborn baby, which is then found, painted, and revived. In other areas he is ritually cut open from neck to groin and relieved of all his insides, which are then replaced with magical substances. However much the pattern may vary, in all instances his supernatural powers are acquired only after an ordeal which he victoriously survives.

Elkin (1977, 172), who calls them "men of high degree," feels that with the revitalization of Aboriginal identity in the 1970s the role of the medicine-men has stabilized. Some of the natives believe them to be superior to the doctors and nurses of the Flying Doctor Services, in that the latter have to rely upon aeroplanes, whereas the former can fly through the air without any of these man-made devices.

However therapeutic the medicine-men have proved to be for the Aborigines, none of them has ever become the kind of charismatic leader who would strip his people of one defunct identity and weld them to another one by his emotional pull. This contrasts sharply with the many charismatic leaders who have emerged amongst the Maoris in New Zealand and other areas of the Pacific. Personal rebirth, or conversion to a new role was typical, but social regeneration was absent altogether.

3. Churinga and Sacred Sites

Awe and reverence are strong sentiments which make the focus of identity more sacred (Mol, 1976, 220). In Aboriginal society strong feelings of awe are attached to the symbols of totemic ancestors, the bull-roarer and the *churinga*. Bull-roarers are wooden objects twirled to make awe-inspiring noises, said to be the "voices" of the ancestors. The *churinga* (an Aranda term) is the more general word for sacred, symbolic objects. A bull-roarer would be a *churinga*, but not all *churingas* are bull-roarers. They are generally engraved or plain wooden boards, symbolizing The Dreaming, but they can also be of stone.

The sight of these *churingas* stirs the deepest feelings of reverence, akin to those experienced by the faithful when contemplating the Blessed Sacrament in some Christian churches. . . . I know of nothing more impressive than to see a group of Aborigines sitting in a secret ground contemplating their sacred symbols and chanting the song versions of the myths appertaining to them (Elkin, 1974, 208).

Similarly, sacred sites are held in great awe. Ancestors are considered to dwell in these places. Despoliation of the sites is the same as killing the ancestors and therefore arouses vehement reactions by those clans and tribes which regard themselves as owners of these sites. Their identity is closely bound to the sites.

4.   Love

In many religions a spirit of love and affection is encouraged and legitimated as a force for the healing and reconciling of precarious identities. In Aboriginal society moral injunctions, particularly those relevant for marriage rules and clan regulations, are also sanctioned by religion. Yet love does not figure in the rules. And so White (1975, 135) observes: "I have never witnessed any public display of affection, not even holding hands, between sexually mature persons of opposite sex, whether married or not."

Erotic love, on the other hand, has functions in Aboriginal society which to Western societies are rather strange. In the West sexual intercourse generally strengthens the husband-wife relationship alone. In Aboriginal society sexual intercourse is used to cement other unions as well.

Elkin (1974, 160ff.) enumerates six of these unions. (1) The unity of a dangerous revenge expedition is sometimes sealed by the temporary exchange of wives. (2) A party about to be attacked sends some of its women to the attackers to indicate that they want to settle peacefully. If the attackers have intercourse with the women, the issue is thereby resolved. (3) In North-Eastern South Australia tribal quarrels about debts are settled by a temporary exchange of wives. (4) The same exchange takes place between groups wanting to consolidate peace and friendship, even when this means a temporary suspension of tribal marriage laws. Incest laws, however, are never broken. (5) The effectiveness of some religious rites, expressing unity, is often thought to improve by sexual intercourse in pre-arranged places. (6) Wives are sometimes loaned to visitors as a token of friendship and hospitality.

In all these instances women are used as a convenience to establish other than marital bonds. The strong feelings aroused by sexual love are thereby channelled in directions which would do harm to the cohesion of the nuclear family in industrialized societies. Yet in societies where socialization takes place in the clan the weakening of exclusive marital bonds is obviously seen as less important. Here too, however, the "sexual act symbolizes commitment, self-giving, and the union of opposites—elements crucial for the cohesion and survival of any social unit" (Mol, 1976, 156).

5. Asceticism

Asceticism, like sacrifice, is an important means of clarifying personal priorities and purifying one's loyalties (ibid., 229). It involves strengthening one commitment at the expense of another. It delineates the priorities and anchors them in the emotions. As asceticism nearly always means renunciation of appetites of one sort or another, the "higher" loyalties are reinforced whenever self-denial is required. And since human nature is indissolubly bound up with appetites, a denial of these appetites is an ever-recurring decision for the ascetic. The ascetic has to encounter cravings of one kind or another with correspondingly stronger commitments to the goal (whether salvation or conquest). This makes asceticism a formidable ally of social discipline.

Durkheim (1965, 351ff.) detects a good deal of asceticism in Aboriginal religion. Indeed, he detects more than there actually is: all his examples are taken from the rather infrequent initiation rites. He could have strengthened his argument if he had included food taboos as comparable instances of ascetic attitudes.

There is, of course, asceticism aplenty in the initiation rites. Neophytes have to abstain from all kinds of food. Of the few things they can eat only the bare minimum is to be consumed. In some tribes they have to beg for food. They are deprived of sleep. They have to refrain from speaking. They cannot wash. And sometimes they are not even allowed to move.

Durkheim explains all this as a necessity for leaving the profane and approaching the sacred. Suffering means detaching oneself from the clutches of the profane. It is a necessary school to subdue our nature and to acquire qualities of disinterestedness and endurance (ibid., 355). Society is possible only at the price of our natural appetites. Therefore religious asceticism advances social solidarity (356).

Only society is sacred in Durkheim's analysis. And this poses a problem. The profane is identified with the non-social or the greedy self. Contrasting forms of sacredness are inadmissable in Durkheim's framework. Therefore, the anti-social stances of sectarian movements, for instance, are, by definition, non-religious. Or self-realization as the sacred principle of humanism cannot be sacred, in spite of the solemn commitments it engenders in humanists and psychoanalysts alike.

Another problem with Durkheim's analysis is that theory and example do not fit. The initiation ceremonies are clearly intended to make a man out of the boy. Manhood, the social, and the sacred are not anymore synonymous with one another than boyhood, the non-social, and the profane are. It makes much more sense to think of the deprivations as sophisticated psychological mechanisms to ease the transition from one encrusted pattern (boyhood) to another (manhood), both of which have their distinct, and even sacralized niche in Aboriginal society. It is true that through the secrecy cults the males can strongly sacralize manhood, but then females have their own totem and so does each individual child.

The asceticism of the initiation rites is therefore, above all, the means to forcibly relativize (and actually destroy) the strongly encrusted puerile identity in order to substitute a male identity for it. How this is done will be elaborated in the section on rites in the next chapter. Here it suffices to stress that asceticism is indeed used (as Durkheim correctly surmised) to stifle adolescent rebellion in order to promote social cohesion indirectly. Yet the temporary ascetic qualities are required only in the specific instance of transition from dependent boyhood to independent manhood. Aboriginal society cannot be called ascetic by any stretch of the imagination. Its problem is rather the reverse: it has been too ready to exchange its social identity for the pottage of Western consumer goods.

In a more general vein: society is never woven of one cloth, not even as primitive a society as the Aboriginal one. Any society contains internally competing forms of sacred and semi-sacred patterns. The variety of totems are adequate proof of this observation. Therefore a good deal of emotion and commitment is required for the maintenance of these patterns. In addition, the relations between these various forms of identity have to be monitored. Asceticism is one way of allocating commitments according to the saliency of competing identities. It can indeed be used for enhancing social cohesion, but it can also be used for enhancing the cohesion of a subversive political movement (whether ultra-left or ultra-right). In Aboriginal society the deprivations associated with initiation are the means for creating a mentality congenial to the implanting of the manhood identity. Yet that identity is not always harmoniously intertwined with others, such as the family or female identity.

6. Sacrifice

Like asceticism, sacrifice can be looked upon as a form of commitment that reinforces a system of meaning or an identity by clarifying priorities. In other words, an impoverished native (non-Australian, I may add—Aborigines do not have sacrifices of this kind) sacrificing a valuable animal to his god thereby commits himself to the god (and the identity he orders) as of greater value than the full stomachs of his family.

Durkheim (1965) has a large section on sacrifice in Aboriginal society. His examples are again exclusively taken from a specific set of rituals, this time totemic ceremonies. During these ceremonies men open veins in their arms, or pierce the skin of their scrotum or navel, in order to make the rite more effective. They believe that blood animates the embryos of the totem animals or plants with which they identify. Following these celebrations, the taboos about eating or even touching the totem become stricter, "as though the sacred character of the totem were reinforced" (ibid., 374). In a final ceremony, several months later, the ritual leader solemnly partakes of the totem. The older men do the same, after which the exceptional taboos are lifted.

Durkheim then explains the sacrifice as collective renovation (ibid., 390) or, as we would say, as a sacralization of clan identity. The members commune together and therefore feel stronger. Durkheim is aware of the renunciation, but does not know very well what to do with it: "every attempt to deduce one of these elements [communion and renunciation] from the other is hopeless" (385). His scheme does not allow him to think in terms of conflicting wholes (self and society). Social regeneration goes hand in hand with individual regeneration (ibid.).

Yet communion and renunciation fit together as soon as one posits conflicts between identities. For then a gain in social cohesion (communion) must accompany a loss (sacrifice) somewhere else. The Aborigine who opens his veins (and there is quite a lot of vein-opening and blood-spattering in Aboriginal rites) thereby solemnly gives priority to the totem (or clan) over his own self. The giving of lifeblood is like saying: "I surrender part of my selfhood (or natural assertiveness, aggression, arrogance, satisfaction of personal appetites, and so forth) to the common good (which requires humility, self-giving, altruism, self-denial)."

Sacrifice of blood in totemic ceremonies therefore means retracing the groove around clan-identity at the expense of the diminishing self. It was the conflict between the self and the social which Durkheim could not very well admit, because it would have led to too much dialectical (as opposed to linear) thinking—and Durkheim's Gallic logic would have suffered. Consequently the social-solidarity model of religion is incomplete. It lacks the subtlety to account *both* for the sacralization of conflicting identities *and* for the religious task of minimizing friction.

Commitment or loyalty is very much present in the other categories (objectification, ritual, and myth) of our analysis. All the categories overlap to an extent. And yet treating them separately has the advantage of keeping certain elements (such as, in this case, emotional anchorage) in the forefront of our thinking about religious phenomena. In this chapter, therefore, we have highlighted the feeling of awe in the presence of *churingas*, feelings of dread in the face of taboos, the feelings of union aroused by sexual intercourse, or the remarkably absent feelings of loyalty to a leader. We have also drawn attention to the orderly distribution of these feelings of attachment to competing identities and meaning-systems through asceticism and sacrifice.

All these feelings have a potent effect on a sense of belonging. Social consensus would not be possible without them. They attach man to the familiar and the predictable. Therefore they are an antidote to the lurking danger of chaos, never far away in any society, and especially not in the Aboriginal one.

4

Ritual

Rites retrace the grooves around order. They strengthen its form and affirm its boundaries. The latter tend to be self-perpetuating. And so the familiar grooves are retraced because familiarity breeds confidence. A particular form of identity may lose some, or even most, of its relevance and yet be perpetuated for its own sake.

Aboriginal society knew (and knows—tradition has not been entirely eroded) a large variety of rites. Some of them, such as the totem ceremonies, retrace the outlines of clan, tribal, and other identities. But others, such as the rites of passage (birth, marriage, initiation, death) strip away an old and weld a new identity in order to safeguard the larger context. We shall consider each of these in turn.

1. Totemic Ceremonies

In these rites (often called corroborees) the performers are usually decorated so as to suggest an actual animal, plant, or event. Thus the performer who is the wildcat trails a long grass cord representing the animal's tail. Or the main performer in the emu clan has a head-dress representing the long neck and head of the emu. The men are generally decked out in patterns of down glued onto their skins with human blood. Intricate patterns of red and yellow ochre may be painted on the yet-uncovered parts of their bodies. All these patterns have symbolic meaning. Circles may represent frogs, and lines on the thighs, frog's legs. But in other totemic ceremonies red string may represent thunder, the white longitudinal bands, lightning, and the black strains, rain falling from the sky (Spencer and Gillen, 1912, vol. 2, 278).

The ceremonial ground is sometimes arranged according to a definite pattern, with earth scooped out or heaped up in the shape of a snake. Intricate designs in the sand symbolize ancestral events. Branches decorate the side. The performers may appear from behind bushes and act out a myth related to their totem. They "are supposed to represent the ancestors and to behave as they did and be decorated as they were in the Alcheringa (Dreaming)," say Spencer and Gillen (ibid., 268), describing Aranda rituals. They may prance around, quiver like the wind, wriggle like a worm, leap like a kangaroo, or snap like a crocodile. Sometimes eating the totem animal or plant is part of the rite.

The audience may consist of males only (many rites are secret) or of women and children as well. The people often participate by dancing, stamping, and shouting. Or they form a sinuous line imitating the snake.

The purpose of these rites is sometimes said to encourage the increase of the totem animal or plant. However, the animals (e.g., lice) are not always useful. Nor are totem events (e.g., cold weather) particularly desirable. It is therefore more likely that totemic rituals remind the clan members who they are and what they represent. The rituals most often sharpen the outline of the clan's identity. Yet it should be remembered that social organization and physical nature are undifferentiated in Aboriginal culture. The wholeness and prosperity of the one is also the wholeness and prosperity of the other.

2.   Rites of Passage

Rites of passage differ from other rites in that they are more complex and comprehensive. Only in the last and third phase do they reinforce a particular identity, as totemic rites do.

There are generally two other phases preceding them. The first strips away or detaches the old pattern, and the second represents the in-between, or "limbo," situation, when the old is obliterated and the new is not yet born. These earlier phases prepare for the changeover from an old to a new identity. They "debrief" or detach emotionally.

In most societies there are at least four of these rites of passage: birth, initiation, marriage, and death. In Aboriginal society birth and marriage rites are of little importance, but initiation and burial make up for them.

3. Birth

Birth affects the familiar grooves of family life by introducing a new member who needs attention, care, and affection. In Aboriginal society the identity of the new member is recognized at the moment the mother becomes aware that she is expecting. Aboriginals think that it is about that time that the pre-existent spirit-child dwelling in a particular location has entered her. The spirit-child may also be hidden in the animal or plant which the mother was eating when she became aware of the pregnancy. This location, animal, plant, or event then becomes the personal totem of the child. In other areas of Australia (e.g., the Great Victoria Desert) the infant's totem depends on the location of its birth rather than its conception (Berndt and Berndt, 1977, 236).

Sometimes the event of conception or birth is suitably demarcated as especially significant. In one tribe (the Unmatjera, north of Alice Springs in Central Australia) the husband "sings" to the wife's navel to make the child grow. He also rubs her sides with grease while chanting words said to have originated in The Dreaming. To the north of the Unmatjera, the Kaitish tribe involve the maternal grandparents in the birth rite. The wife's father touches his daughter's head with a twig, and then the grandmother rubs the baby across her stomach and throws it up and down in the air. Meanwhile, the baby's father has absented himself from the camp for three days, but has left his waist-girdle and arm-bands behind to guarantee a beneficial birth. On his return he "warms a spearthrower over the fire and passes it backwards and forwards over the child's body, after which he paints a circle of black around the eyes and the naval" (Spencer and Gillen, 1904, 607).

The Warramunga (around Tennant Creek to the north of the Kaitish) insist that the child be born in a special camp of female relations, while close male relations, such as her husband and father, are under a ban of silence. A week after the birth, the mother carries the child to her husband's camp. He presents it with weapons, after which the ban of silence is lifted. Separation from the normal location, the silence of the in-between period, the acceptance of the baby are typical for a rite of passage.

For other Australian tribes, there is, unfortunately, very little information about birth rites.

4. Marriage

The marriage ceremonies which have been reported by investigators are informal and simple. In Central Australia the female initiation rite or defloration is simultaneously a marriage rite. After the operation the man who carried it out "decorates her with furstring, rat-tails, etc. and takes her to the camp of her allotted husband, to whom she then belongs" (Spencer and Gillen, 1904, 134). Puberty rituals and marriage are also linked in the Flinders Range of South Australia. A few days after initiation the bride is led to the camp of the future husband and seated next to him. Two glowing fire sticks are laid on the ground in front of the couple. To the assembled crowd it is then explained that the fire is the couple's fire "and that they must live together beside it and not desert it for that of anyone else" (Mountford and Harvey, 1941, 162). Berndt and Berndt (1977, 200) explain that one of the sticks is a grooved "hearthstick" and the other the drill stick for twirling in it—"symbolically, female and male, complementary in the process of fire-making."

In the Kimberleys (Western Australia) marriage rites begin with the husband taking his girl by the arm and disappearing into the bush for a few days. There they paint themselves with red ochre and on their return are presented by the girl's parents with spears, handkerchiefs, and other articles. She is given hill-kangaroo, wildcat, and a small kind of iguana, all foods which were taboo until marriage (Kaberry, 1939, 94).

The relative insignificance of the marriage rite in Aboriginal society may have a number of reasons.

1.   The universal betrothal or bestowal custom determines long in advance (and long before at least one of the partners is of marriageable age) who is to marry whom. Marriage is not a sudden break. Nor is there much change in sexual habits. Aboriginal society is rather permissive and there is much premarital experimentation. Yet one would therefore expect the transition to a more enduring relationship and greater fidelity to be important.

2.   The break with the family in which husband and wife have grown up has already been made. Therefore the threat of competitive attachments for the new marital bond is small. In Aboriginal society there is much stress on the initiation rites. These are rites which, par excellence, prepare men and women for adult independence. Initiation rites are compensatory in this respect. The detachment or stripping-away phase of marriage becomes less important as a consequence of the strong emphasis on this phase in initiation ceremonies.

3.   Males regard marriage as a business transaction in which simple economic values are exchanged (i.e., the provisionary abilities of sisters given in marriage to another clan against those of wives received in return). This attitude tends to decrease the importance of the marital bond as such.

4. A system of taboos regarding marital behaviour and relations with in-laws safeguards the elementary family on a day-to-day basis from interference and dependence.

5. Many of the socialization functions of the family are carried out by the clan.

Yet in varying degrees these betrothal customs, initiation ceremonies, male attitudes, and marital taboos exist in other societies with fully developed marriage ceremonies. It could be that one should not always assume a close-fitting religious legitimation of all identities or all important units of a given social system.

On the other hand, the frequent elopements, divorces, abandonments, and family quarrels in Aboriginal society may point to a precariousness and weakness which could have been offset by stronger legitimations, sanctions, and taboos. One certainly wonders whether the intricate dialectic between femininity and masculinity is not overly slanted in the male direction, to the detriment of family stability.

5. Initiation

Initiation ceremonies illustrate the principle behind rites of passage: the stripping (in this case, of adolescents) from one identity and the welding to a new one (in this case manhood). Social unity is maintained by guiding and mitigating the inevitable change from the dependent child to the independent adult. In contrast with charismatic leadership, rites of passage guide potentially disorderly change *within* the social system rather than potentially disorderly

Initiation throughout Australia begins with separation from the familiar camp and motherly protection. It is a forceful and fearful demarcation from a happy, permissive past in which the novice was often spoiled, cuddled, and dominated by females. In the Western Desert a boy, if he is the youngest child, "is likely to sleep in his mother's embrace until he leaves for the bachelor's camp at the age of twelve or thirteen" (White, 1975, 134).

There is much wailing on the part of the women when the novices are torn away from them. The Wiradthuri tribes (South-Central New South Wales) cover the women, children, and novices with rugs when it is announced that the sky-spirit and initiator, Daramulun, is on the way. His arrival is accompanied by an unholy din: bull-roarers make their awesome sound, the ground is beaten with strips of bark, and there is much stamping and throwing of fire sticks. When the women and children are uncovered, they find that the novices have noiselessly disappeared (their guardians have led them away). It is explained to them that Daramulun tried to burn the boys when he took them away and the half burnt pieces of wood are shown as evidence (Matthews, 1896, 308).

The secret myth which accompanies this part of the proceedings is equally bone chilling. Daramulun was originally charged by Baiame, the sky-being, to carry out the initiations. His job consisted of taking the novices away into the bush and teaching them all the laws, traditions, and customs of the tribe. To do that "he always killed the boys, cut them up, burnt them to ashes, formed the ashes into human shape, and restored them to life, new beings, but each with a tooth missing" (ibid., 297). In a parallel myth he was said to swallow the boys and to vomit them up after a time, now possessing all the tribal knowledge, but minus a tooth.

However, Daramulun was too zealous and Baiame had to discharge him, so that the elders had to carry out the initiations on his behalf. Daramulun was so ferocious that while wrenching out the tooth of the novices with his own teeth, he would devour the whole boy. Baiame became suspicious when too many of the novices went missing and decided that Daramulun had just gone a bit too far. Yet the latter's voice is still heard whenever the bull-roarer swings during the rites.

The tribes of South-East Queensland start initiation proceedings by taking the novices away from their mothers. The latter, however, follow them, until they are chased away with spears. The boys are further removed, but are then told: "Your mothers are calling you, run off to them." This they promptly do, until they are intercepted by armed men hidden in the scrub (Matthews, 1911, 107).

In South-Western Arnhem land the Murimbata initiation ceremonies similarly begin with the forceful separation of the novices. The mothers give a heart-rending wail, reminding one of the death of a relation. Here, too, the youths must be treated as dead; their names can no longer be mentioned.

Instead of Daramulun and Baiame it is Karwadi, the Mother of All, the Old Woman, living in the deep waters, who presents herself with the roar of the bull-roarer. She has come to swallow the boys alive and then vomit them up again. Here, too, separation is crucial for the ceremony. The novices cannot show themselves during the day. They have to wait until late at night before they are allowed to sneak back into the camp, and they have to leave again before the camp stirs. They cannot wash and have to sleep caked with blood from head to foot (Stanner, 1966, 8). Separation is so important, in fact, that it is repeated like the theme in a Bach fugue. After a number of days, when the boys have been given a forehead band, a hairbelt, a necklace, and a genital covering (clearly marks of re-integration), they are humbled again by being ordered to crawl under the spread legs of men from the opposite moiety. At the end of the line each of the boys "sits momentarily in front of his mother, with his back to her, but not touching or touched by her, while all the women wail and lacerate their heads to draw blood" (ibid., 9). Then they return between the legs of the immobile men. This confrontation and second separation from their mothers reinforces the earlier episode. Yet this time the separation is not forcible and passive. It is an active participation (symbolic voluntariness) on the part of the novices, making their independence all the more definite. The return to the boys' mothers in the middle of the ceremonies is also mentioned for other tribes, for instance, the Wonggumuk in Central Victoria (Matthews, 1905, 877).

Stanner (1966, 138) interprets this return as an independent phase and wants to insert it chronologically between the second (transitional) and third (integrative) phase. Yet in our model of interpretation it is a re-emphasis of what we have called the detaching or identity-stripping sequence, in order to delineate the past from the present even more strongly.

Liminality, lostness, or meaninglessness is always clearly present in the Australian rites of initiation. It is the episode when suggestibility is at a maximum. A sharply different identity can only grow when the old soil has been thoroughly uprooted and the new plant has minimum competition. Old attachments may have to be pruned drastically before new attachments can be grafted on. This is as true for brainwashing as it is for college hazing, Christian conversion, and paradigm change in science.

It is also true of Aboriginal initiation. No attempt is spared to make the detachment from the former existence real. What the novices used to do (speak, eat, or sleep) is now forbidden. In some instances guards stand watch to make sure that the boys do not doze off in the night. And what was forbidden is now prescribed. The Keeparra (East coast of New South Wales from Newcastle to the Macleay River) give their initiands portions of human excrement to eat and urine to drink while the bull-roarers produce an eerie thunder (Matthews, 1897, 331). The Walloonggurra (North-East coast of New South Wales) rub their genitals on the food which is given to the boys (Matthews, 1900, 69). The world has all of a sudden become an upside-down world. Yet the utter confusion is a prerequisite for the rebirth. It is this dying and being reborn which the Walbiri (Western Desert of Northern Territory) equate with circumcision (Meggitt, 1962, 294). Other tribes make the initiands crouch in a trench representing the womb of the Mother (Hallam, 1975, 95), thus symbolizing both their present non-existence and their future birth. The rebirth theme in initiation is also stressed by Berndt and Berndt (1977, 220, for instance) and Eliade (1973, 99ff.).

The Murimbata novice, too, is treated as a naked, nameless nothing. In his circumcision ceremony the boy is taken completely out of the familiar environment of kin and clan. For as long as two months, the guardian (again a future-in-law from another clan) takes him to unfamiliar country amongst strangers and puts him "under a severe, if kindly discipline: a scrupulous observance of many food taboos, a sparing use of water, a modest demeanour, and a deferential attention to his instructors" (Stanner, 1966, 113). In the later, Karwadi ceremony, the circle receiving the novices continuously mimes the blow-fly, which habitually settles on rotting flesh.

In Central Australia the novice is treated rather roughly. He is thrown in the air and generally ill-treated. If he is obnoxious and not docile enough, the punishment is suitably increased. A painful bite on the scalp is one of the ways to increase the initiand's misery. Extraction of fingernails is another (Strehlow, 1970, 116).

In South-East Australia the boys are made to walk over hot coals left from the fire. Some of the coals are shoved on leafy boughs, which then are shaken over the novices. In other ceremonies the boys are made to do senseless things, such as throwing dirt or engaging in the very thing they feel least like doing, such as childish pranks.

All this of course, does not offset the actual fear and physical pain of hair-plucking, tooth avulsion, circumcision, subincision, and cicatrization (producing a pattern of raised scars by means of cutting the skin and rubbing foreign matter in the wound). These procedures are not always carried out, but at least one of them is generally part of initiation ceremonies and adds substantially to the anxiety and apprehension so typical of this middle phase.

The foundation for the last and final phase (the welding of the new identity) is laid in the early beginnings of the rite. It is the spirit of affection and fellowship which the initiators establish with the initiands. They protect the boys against the ferocious incursions of the sky-spirits. Daramulun attempts to burn the Wiradthuri boys, but their guardians shield them. Or Goign (the sky-spirit of the Keeparra, who has aspirations of an equally evil kind), is put off the track: "The boys are not here yet" (Matthews, 1897, 331). As the novices cannot speak, the guardians must attend to their needs by guessing sympathetically what they want and help them. The blood which covers the Murimbata youths is commonly the blood of their initiators, as though the latter, being their potential wife's brothers, have both a stake in their independent manhood and in their safety. Only they can speak to the initiands.

What are the new values and attitudes welded into initiated manhood? It would be excessively harsh and overly bold to say that the major new set of attitudes deals with the active manipulation of women. This is certainly not overtly the case. Nor do Aboriginal men fit the stereotype of the caveman who clubs the female into submission and tames her to cater to all his needs and desires. There is too much natural affection between men and women in Aboriginal society to justify this brutal picture. Also, the indubitable termination of the phase of being dominated by women (which the rites certainly are about) does not necessarily herald the opposite phase of dominating them. In addition, values such as courage, determination, and capacity to cope with pain and anxiety (all strongly encouraged values) are not exclusively masculine.

And yet, there is enough latent truth in the idea not to dismiss it too hastily. After all, the ceremonies bind the initiates together in a society, of which the secret lore is too lofty for inferiors such as women and children. The latter have to remain in the mistaken illusion that Daramulun or Karwadi rather than the elders carry out the initiation, even though the former has been dismissed by Baiame and the latter is dead. They are never to be told, on pain of death, that the bull-roarers are swung by men rather than sky-gods and water deities.

The manhood which the initiation sacralizes is now more clearly delineated from womanhood. Secrecy strongly enhances identity. Delineation is not only intransitive, it is also transitive. It is, moreover, a delineation from its logical opposite, womanhood. And as Strehlow (1968, 93) reminds us for Central Australia, women may be the owners of the most sacred *churinga* of their clan and yet be deliberately excluded from such important knowledge.

It is of course true that the secret lore, the ancient traditions of The Dreaming, the sacred *churingas*, and the bull-roarers form an independent meaning-system. They relate the initiate to a world order straddling social divisions and functions. They do *not* narrowly advocate a masculine view of the world. The objectifications provided by the Baiame, Goign, Daramulun, and Karwadi cults straddle a more differentiated universe than the totems do. Stanner is right when he stresses that the prime motive of the Karwadi ceremony is the "continuation of a plan of life, given once-and-for-all in The Dreaming, but in continuous danger of corruption by those who in the course of nature must carry it on" (1966, 4). Or as he says further, the rites "deal with the whole of reality" (27). "The novice is a man transformed into a man of mystical understanding, a man who knows the truth" (30).

Yet an objectified meaning-system can provide a wider order for a variety of identities. And obviously its being confined to initiates makes it irrelevant for anybody else. The cults and the totems served a different clientele or unit of social organization. Therefore they often happily co-existed, as it were, in separate boxes of the memory bank of the same personnel.

In a relatively undifferentiated society it is less necessary to connect all these boxes and provide the rationalizations for their interconnections. In such a system of rationalizations the abstractions proferred by the sky-spirit idea, however, offer opportunities not provided by the totemic principle. Potentially (but the potentiality is thwarted by cult secrecy), the former can lead to distinctive transcendental delineations for the ordering of the "boxes" vis-à-vis one another.

The upshot of all this is that we have to temper Stanner's interpretation by insisting that the initiation ceremonies of the Murimbata contained a considerable, though latent, sacralization of manhood as separate and distinct.

It is for similar reasons that Elkin's rather Durkheimian interpretation of the rites must be modified. His argument is simple: the ceremonies link the initiate to the tribe; they develop his social personality and widen his interests to the whole group. The rites therefore "create and renew feelings and experiences of social unity and cohesion; they ensure respect for the tribe's moral and social sanctions" (Elkin, 1974, 213). Elkin would answer the question for this section (what are the specific attitudes and beliefs which are welded into the new identity?) in a very simple way: the only identity worth considering is the tribal one, and the ceremony encourages those values which reinforce this larger unity. Manhood contributes to social cohesion. The co-operation of opposing moieties in initiation is further evidence that tribal cohesion is the central issue. He would probably add to this argument that this co-operation is rather similar to the increase rites carried out in Central Australia by one clan for the benefit of the others.

Yet this view is too simple. The initiation ceremonies do *not* neatly dovetail in a harmonious social structure. If tribal cohesion were all that mattered, a conflicting set of beliefs about important happenings in The Dreaming would not be tolerated, for the initiates now have to practice hypocrisy, as false beliefs have to be reinforced when they talk with women and true ones when they speak with fellow initiates.

Another aspect of the initiation ceremony also throws doubt on the picture of tribal harmony. Stanner describes the wild licence of the Tjirmumuk, an indispensable part of the Murimbata ceremonies.

It consists of ritualized horseplay between the moieties participating in the initiation. "Men who stand to each other as cross-cousins, wife's brothers, wife's fathers and mothers' brothers, push and jostle one another, snatch away small personal possessions, pluck at each others' genitals, and in a laughing voice shout things which would ordinarily be obscene, embarrassing, and hurtful . . . ." Stanner then goes on to say that the Tjirmumuk is not to the Aborigines an act of profanation, but part of the rite as a whole. He objects to the Durkheimian distinction between the sacred and the profane as too simple and not true to the facts. He describes the Tjirmumuk as a "negative affirmation of what was affirmed positively in the first phase, as a replacing of solemnity by ribaldry, altruism by hostility and solidarity by opposition" (64). In other words, the sacred and tribal solidarity do not mesh.

In our terms, the Tjirmumuk may be a self-corrective device in the larger context. It appears to delineate what the other part tended to obfuscate: the distinction between the moieties. Until the Tjirmumuk, co-operation between the moieties was embarrassingly close. The initiator's blood was even sacrificed for boys of the opposing side. And yet the function of a moiety is opposition in the intricate system of marital taboos. Or, as Burridge (1973, 136-37) reminds us: "moiety systems . . . formed opposed but complementary categories for ceremonial and ritual purposes." The Tjirmumuk therefore seems to be a counterbalance to dysfunctional closeness.

Summarizing our argument: the complex of initiation rites delineates an intricate pattern of congruent and conflicting identities. However, delineation is only part of the complex. The rites also facilitate potentially disruptive transitions between these identities. They strip away emotional attachments to one identity and weld new attachments to another. In other words, they affirm order and minimize the formless void of chaos and disorder. The latter they do by means of guiding the unavoidable change of adolescence to adulthood.

6. Death

To the Australian Aborigine death meant transition from normal being to mobile spirit. The latter could be here, there, and everywhere, if you were not careful. Eventually this spirit would settle again in the ancestral Dreaming. At least this is what a considerable number of Aborigines vaguely assumed to be the case.

Much can be said about the intricate "fit" of beliefs about death in a system of values and meanings. The hereafter becomes important when continuity of values becomes a necessity. Even more could be said about the psychology of scapegoating (blaming enemies for a perfectly natural death) or of pain infliction (to balance grief). However, here we are concerned with rites of death and burial.

These rites are rites of transition. Yet transition here has a social rather than a personal meaning. They guide the changeover from a disrupted group or social identity to a re-integrated one. The feverish restoration by the spider of the gash in his web comes to mind by way of comparison. In both cases a partial breakdown is offset by an amended wholeness.

Yet the comparison fails in that death rites, like all other rites of passage, deal rather decisively with *emotional* detachment and re-attachment. And I do not know of any study dealing with the blood pressure of the spider when his web is interfered with! With humans there is no doubt about that aspect. And therefore the rites manfully articulate the separation or tear in the social fabric, come to grips with it in the expression of a sense of loss and deep grief, and heal the wounds through acts of communion, or singing and dancing on the grave, as the Bathurst Islanders do.

Before we take each of these three phases in turn, it should be made clear what we do *not* mean. Similarity in basic design and purpose of the rites of passage does *not* mean similarity of content. The rites of passage involve hair-plucking, tooth avulsion, circumcision, subincision, cicatrization, and so forth. Yet whatever the difference in content, all of them had in common a stripping away and a welding of identity.

The same applies here. Death rites in Aboriginal society may vary all the way from cremation, mummification, tree burial, and grave burial, to cannibalism. Yet they all have in common a basic design of emotional detachment and re-attachment to the salient units of social organization.

This means that historical speculation as to the derivation of Aboriginal initiation ceremonies from burial ones is rather irrelevant. Both are branches of a more basic process and therefore neither is derived from the other. Nor does a comparison of content, such as knocking out the tooth of the initiate, representing "the ritual opening of the mouth of the corpse, that the deceased may eat and drink and so live" (Elkin, 1974, 199), make sense. The concrete shape of the symbol may be as varied as the numerous totems, and the basic symbol behind the concretization may lie only loosely behind the object, ready "to jump from one carrier to another" (Mol, 1976, 252). What is important is that the basic process has proved to be viable enough to survive both the stone age and the technological revolution. The point is that superficial comparisons may obscure the fundamental functions of the rites under discussion.

We may now consider, one by one, the three phases of stripping away of identity (separation), lack of identity (transition), and welding of identity (re-integration).

6.1 The Separation Phase: Stripping Away of Identity

"Separation" is a better word here. The family, clan, moiety, or tribe is not totally "stripped away"; it is only disrupted, as our spiderweb was, or "stripped" of one of its members. It is this disrupting element (death) which must be excised to prevent festering. Festering would weaken the family or the clan as a going concern.

The wound which death has made in the body politic can be insignificant or serious. Australian Aboriginal burial rites roughly reflect the significance or insignificance of the person dying. The most elaborate ritual is reserved for the promising leader in his prime. Women rate a decidedly lesser funeral, while infants or very old men hardly rate at all.

Yet this is only true for the larger social units (clan, moiety, tribe). For the family, close attachments determine the decibel count of wailing and the amount of blood produced by gashing and cutting. However, that there is in fact such a decisive variation in treatment, according to place in the clan rather than according to attachments within the family, should caution us again not to over-estimate the place of the elementary family in Aboriginal society. It would be interesting to know whether the wailing of close relatives varies with the position of the dead person in the social structure. In Central Australia the more mortal of the two souls of man was supposed to hover balefully around the place where the body had died, keenly watching the "surviving members of its late community, drawing comfort from the show of deep sorrow made by its late relatives and friends . . ." (Strehlow, 1964, 739).

The separating or excising rites are numerous. The camp is often moved to another site. The name of the deceased becomes taboo. Sometimes all his or her possessions (which one should not overestimate!) are burnt or buried. At other times fire is used to chase the soul away.

The Kakadu (of North-Central Arnhem Land) decontaminate dillybags (for collecting food) and other utensils by hanging them in the smoke from a special fire (Spencer, 1914, 243). Maddock explains many of the death rites as a way of breaking the habit of the spirit "to hang about its former home." The breaking of limbs and disposal of the body make the latter "unattractive to, or unapproachable by its spirit" (1972, 170). Berndt and Berndt mention the rites for sending "the spirit on its way," wherever that may be—the sky, the deep waters, or a hole in the rocks.

Mourning habits are also a prime example of separateness. The difference is that, this time, surviving relatives set themselves apart from the community at large. Through their attachment to the deceased they need special consideration before returning to normality. And so the widows on the Darling River of New South Wales wear helmet-shaped objects, called Kurno, as a special mourning dress. The Kakadu (of North-Central Arnhem Land) paint themselves with black for deep mourning and white for half mourning. Black may change into white in the later ceremonies for at least some of the more distant relatives (Spencer, 1914, 245).

6.2   The Transition Phase: Lack of Identity

The acute sense of loss and the intense grief are well expressed in the wailing and self-mutilation. The emotional detachment from the person with whom one was closely associated is inevitable, but the resulting sense of meaninglessness can also be socially dangerous. The grief-stricken members can lose considerable motivation and thereby jeopardize family or communal order. It is for this reason that loving consolation and communal affection are vital at this period. They are effective antidotes to alienation and anomie.

The expression of the loss felt can take a variety of forms. The widower and sons of a Kakadu woman poured the blood from their self-inflicted wounds into the paper bark in which the body was wrapped (Spencer, 1914, 241). The female relatives of a dead man of the Gnanji (Centre of the Northern Territory) cut their scalps with yam-sticks and seared the wounds with a red-hot fire stick to express their grief. They were also under a strict ban of silence for a considerable time (until the last of a series of burial ceremonies), according to Spencer and Gillen (1904, 545). The Dieri (of North-East South Australia) burn their arms (Howitt, 1904, 465). In other areas, again, thighs are cut.

6.3   The Re-integration Phase: Welding of Identity

This phase has been particularly well documented for the Murngin (of North-East Arnhem Land). It was amongst them that W. Lloyd Warner did his fieldwork from 1926 to 1929. He reported extensive singing and dancing at the various ceremonies. Some of the dances, he said, simulated fights between the living and the dead and some of the songs symbolized change (1964, 423). As part of the rites, food was consumed by the clansmen and the close male relatives of the dead man. Others could (and did) watch this communion but could not participate.

Warner interprets the primary motive for these rites to be "to reintegrate the society, close its ranks after the removal of one of its members, and once more assert its solidarity.... The period of mourning corresponds fairly definitely to the period of readjustment of the social structure to his social loss" (1964, 434).

Earlier evidence for these re-integrative rites come from other parts of Arnhem Land and the surrounding areas. On Melville and Bathurst Island there was much dancing and singing around the wooden graveposts. The closest relatives took the lead at these dances while others participated with furious stamping, keeping perfect time. Various animals were represented in the dance, the crouching crocodile or the browsing, pawing buffalo (Spencer, 1914, 235-36).

The Kakadu have a solemn communion meal of lily-seed cakes, eaten by the older men, at the end of the second burial ceremony (ibid., 245). In other areas, the Waduman (South-West Arnhem Land) and the Mudburra (adjoining them to the South) eat the clan totem some weeks after the placing of the bones in a tree grave. The women bring in supplies of food and some of the close male relatives of the deceased go out into the bush to capture flying foxes (the totem animal). The cooked foxes are then eaten by selected relatives, after which everyone can eat the totem animal as well as the yams, lily cakes, and other food provided by the women (ibid., 250).

In the same way as birth originates with the spirit-child's looking for a womb, so Aboriginals believe that death, too, has specific non-natural causes. Behind death, they think, there is generally sorcery. They therefore hold inquests to prove or disprove the allegations. These are generally held several days or weeks after the death has occurred. Various signs, all related to the body or the possessions of the deceased, are interpreted as pointing to the guilty person.

It is often the deviant individual, the brazen adulterer, the habitually hateful, the jealous gossip, the arrogant sceptic, the secretive schemer, the former or present enemy, the non-conformist, on whom the suspicion falls. Sorcery and death both point to the relative vulnerability of the social fabric: death and deviancy both contribute to breakdown. Therefore both the funeral rites and the action against sorcerers can be seen as means of restoring wholeness.

Yet this is not the entire story. Sorcery and scapegoating can be psychological compensations for individually experienced pain and frustration. Similarly death rituals have theological and psychological (non-social) ramifications. Nevertheless, they both tend to make up for what a society regards as inevitable breaches of its order.

Myths about death play their own part in the healing of a saddened clan, family, or tribe. They soothe, for instance, through dramatization of the cosmic struggle between life and death.

There are many Aboriginal myths dealing with this theme. The moon, which is always a male in these myths (the sun being the female), figures prominently because it is supposed to be immortal. It disappears but then always returns. The moon, according to a Wotjo (West Victoria) myth was in the habit of raising all men and women from the dead. But then an old man (obviously tired of life himself) said, "Let them remain dead." This is what the moon did, and ever since humans have never come back to life again. Only the moon himself remains eternal.

The Tiwi (of Melville Island) explain death as the result of the anger of one of their ancestors, Purukupali. The latter's wife had a secret lover, Tjapara, a bachelor, and while they were making love she neglected her tiny son, who died of exposure. Purukupali was so angry that he decreed that from that time onward everyone should die (heretofore they had not).Tjapara protested, and a fierce fight broke out between him and Purukupali, which neither won. However, the latter picked up his dead son, backed into the sea, and shouted, "You must all follow me; as I die, so must all of you die." Then the waters closed over his head. Thereupon Tjapara changed himself into the moon, the wounds still visible on his face. "But he did not entirely escape the decree of Purukupali, for, even though Tjapara is eternally reincarnated, he has to die for three days" (Mountford, 1958, 29-30).

There are many more myths dealing with life and death. The telling of these familiar stories in the larger circle of relations and clan members had a reconciling effect on those most immediately involved in a death. However, we will deal with the sacralizing effect of myth more fully in the next chapter.

In summary: death rituals as well as other rites of passage can be classified as involving either the stripping away of an old or the welding of a new or renewed identity. In between these opposing processes is a transitional period of identity loss, which is also clearly delineated.

Yet it would be a mistake to think that all these phases and rites were both equally present and prominent. They were not. There is not enough documentation to assure that all phases of even the prominent rites were actually present. For instance, only for North Australia is there sufficient evidence for the last phase of the death rites. It could quite well be that there was not such a phase elsewhere, or that the daily contacts and primary relations of a tightly knit clan made ritual expression of a *fait accompli* superfluous.

The relative unimportance or even non-existence of birth and marriage rites in certain areas of Australia should also caution us not to expect a one-for-one relationship between life-cycle changes in Aboriginal society and their ritual chaperones. Some of these changes may have been regarded as unimportant, or, if important, as perfectly solvable by other means. On the other hand, the contributions which a clearer delineation of a specific order, such as the elementary family, can make may not have occurred to anyone. Not even a well-integrated society, such as the Aboriginal one, should be regarded as a finely, intricately intermeshed whole. A tendency toward the meshing of a whole is a far cry from its actually being such.

Yet all these cautions do not take away from the important contributions which rituals made to this process of making whole, of identity formation, and of delineation of order.

5

Myths

There is considerable overlap between the provision for order we discussed in chapter two (objectification) and the ordering of myths. Both hold arbitrariness and meaninglessness at bay. Both contribute to the integration of vital elements of existence.

Yet there is also an important difference. In the objectification chapter we stressed the distance between the framework of order and the mundane. Here we will stress the intricate composition and content of the projected order. Objectification, we said, deals with transcendental ordering, and the emphasis was on "transcendental." Myths, on the other hand, deal with recurrent narrations. They integrate the various strains of mundane experience in a symbolic account. They make "explicit or implicit statements about man's place in his environment" (Mol, 1976, 246).

Therefore totems and sky-beings were discussed in chapter two. They strengthened the clan, tribe, moiety, manhood, personhood by linking them with a system of meaning which neither moth nor rust could corrupt. Here, on the other hand, we are more interested in the form of the awe-inspiring narratives about, for instance, the mythical beings of The Dreaming.

Myths were not always viewed in this way. In the nineteenth century scholars of religion, such as Andrew Lang (1906, 4), called them "irrational and debasing." Max Müller (cited in Burridge, 1973, 192) referred to them as a "disease of language." Yet in the first half of the twentieth century Durkheim began to think about them as the perpetuation of tribal memories and traditions, representations of man and the world, "a moral system and a cosmology as well as history" (1965, 420). Malinowski called them a narrative resurrection of a primeval reality and a pragmatic charter of primitive faith and moral wisdom (1954, 101).

The second half of the twentieth century saw yet again an altogether different approach to the study of myths. Lévi-Strauss (1967, 226) viewed myth as a message constructed out of binary oppositions or as crystallizations of diverse cultural elements around a suitable symbolic core.

It is this approach which we will use. Yet we will also go beyond Lévi-Strauss. The bisecting and re-ordering of mythical structures is not enough. It must be complemented by a substantive theme, which in our case is the dialectic of identity/change, integration/differentiation, wholeness/breakdown.

Throughout, our interest has been in the way religion contributes to, and moderates between, a variety of identities. If this contribution is real, it should be visible in the dramatization of the identity/change dialectic. If myths reconcile the perpetual struggle between what makes for wholeness (on any level) and what upsets it, that should be detectable in their woof and warp. Or, even more fundamentally, if religion sacralizes identity, then myths must show this process.

1. Territory

Territorial myths fit like a hand in the glove of our assumptions. We have assumed for good reasons that territorial integrity was as important for *homo sapiens* as it was for many of the primates and other animal species. In addition we have suggested that those human groups which could manage to preserve their territorial integrity, while simultaneously developing an intricate division of labour within their territory, would have the greater potential for survival. Other groups, we said, would lose out in the competition with hordes that were more efficient in the hunt and the defence because of their capacity for internal communication. To maximize the advantages of learning over instinct, a longer protection of children and a more elaborate social organization (particularly the family) would be necessary.

Religion, we have assumed, became universal because it proved to be very adaptive for the maintenance of, and the moderation between, identities. These identities were originally entirely and exclusively territorial but became differentiated in a more organizational and social direction when that direction proved to be more advantageous.

In addition religion proved to have a vital task in keeping rudderless communication at a minimum. It is this task which, I think, religion has never lost from its most primitive origins to its most sophisticated forms in modern technological societies. What I mean by "rudderless communication" is the kind of communication that is haphazard, i.e., does not alternate between a relevant framework of order and the actions necessary for mastering the mundane. Purposeful communication, on the other hand, always relates the objectified system of meaning to instrumental activities. Alienation, anomie, and lack of motivation are the backlash of rudderless communication—a not uncommon phenomenon amongst Aboriginals affected by the West.

In terms of these assumptions we therefore expect that the older and the more primitive a society is the more likely we are to find a close link between territorial integrity and religion. The Aboriginal territorial myths appear to prove the point. They are the oldest and most widespread of all the myths, and yet the least recorded. They are the least appropriate for the universal discourse of scientific investigation. They are relevant only for the specific group of people in the specific territory under consideration. They are boring for everyone else. The waterholes, the mountains, and the other physical characteristics of the landscape are meaningless to anyone but a handful of natives.

Tantalizingly, the scholarly literature refers to them (e.g., in the myths about the Wawilak sisters naming the animals, plants, and clan territories on their journey towards the sea)—but then quickly passes on to things of greater interest to a discriminating reader. In all the recording of myths these references to unfamiliar items of the landscape suffer most in the summaries. Yet there is good evidence that these myths were indeed the most common and the most widespread in Aboriginal society.

Fortunately, a number of anthropologists have carefully recorded them. Particularly, the excellent article by Ronald Berndt (blessed be the Berndts' voluminous productivity and their capacity to get it all into print!) on traditional morality (1970b) contain a whole list, even though the title leads one to expect that the article deals with morality rather than territorial myths.

What does Ronald Berndt say? We will present some selected excerpts of his already-excerpted myths (Berndt, 1970b, 225ff.).

Throughout the North-Western sector of the Western Desert there is a common series of secret sacred myths and rituals called the *dingari*. The mythical beings (also called *dingari*) move across the country in the vicinity of Lake White and erect some of their secret sacred ritual boards (called *darugu*) on a hill and by their power cause fire to issue from the apex of each board. The *dingari* enter the ground at Wilgungara and emerge at Djawuldjawul.

In Berndt's Myth-Section IV the *dingari* begin their travels at Warawara on the Canning Stock Route. There they make *darugu* boards. A kangaroo is frightened by the feathers attached to a *darugu*. The *dingari* perform ritual and make stone-flake blades for spears. They kill two old men with one of their *darugu*, using it as a throwing stick. After hitting them, the *darugu* continues for some distance and finally falls, forming a mountain ridge. The *dingari* follow it and then return home, where they sing, grind grass seeds, and finally mount their *darugu* to fly through the sky to Ngalgildjara soak (swamp).

The mythical beings camp here, throw stones there, eat possum at a third location. In a fourth place they dance a ritual and paint youths with arm-vein blood; there a big creek rises, made by their dancing feet. They fight with an old man, Djilgamada (echidna), who goes under the ground and comes up again some distance away, in Walbiri country. The *dingari* find him again, but he escapes into a rockhole which he makes so large that all of his attackers fall into it.

Eventually, the mythical beings come to Manggi. Here they make a *ganala* trench (symbolizing the womb of Gadjeri, the Old Woman or Mother—similar to Karwadi of the Murimbata). The Gadjeri Mother is here: men enter her belly. As she walks along, her footprints form rows of waterholes (at Rubudjungu). From time to time she permits the men to go out for hunting, but they always return to her.

At this point Berndt (1970b, 236) comments that in the Desert one hears much more about the *dingari* than about Gadjeri, who, "has, as far as we can tell, come into the Desert and been integrated into and adapted to the local socio-cultural environment." This again suggests that the sky-being beliefs are likely to be a later imposition (like a palimpsest) on an older totemic, localized tradition. It also suggests that in the newer tradition the basic opposition between the integrative (Gadjeri) and the instrumental (hunting) begins to be articulated.

The point about the territorial myths is clear. They are prime examples of identity sacralization. What is more, "all Desert myths are territorially anchored and are therefore in the possession of those people who claim particular stretches of country" (Berndt, 1970b, 233).

Two other points have to be made. The first is that territorial myths will have to expand to incorporate newcomers to the home country. Mythical links have to be established in order to validate the incorporation of one group with another. Elkin (1974, 60) calls this the growing-up of a mythology.

The other point is that the close linkage of territorial and social identity requires the articulation of the transcendental unity binding them. The myths of origin, to which we now turn, meet this requirement.

2. Order/Disorder Myths

Aboriginals often explain mundane change or disorder in terms of mythical events at The Dreaming. The latter does not just represent order, which contains and tames disorder from a distance, as it were, but locates that disorder at its own heart.

Warner (1964, 375) quotes his informants as saying: "The cycle of the seasons with the growth and decay of vegetation, copulation, birth and death of animals as well as man, is all the fault of those Wawilak sisters." The latter are ancestral beings whose heinous sins—to be related in the rebirth myths—are responsible for death and change.

This is reminiscent of Stanner's stress on the paradox of human impairment and the unity of The Dreaming. The Murimbata myths present an intuited dualism (Stanner, 1966, 155) or antinomy common to all structures of existence (167). "In several important myths the dominant theme was an irreparable injury to man at the beginning of life under instituted forms" (ibid.). Aborigines "saw themselves as the heirs of a cracked estate" (164).

The Dreaming connected the parts divided by strife (ibid.) or to express this in our terms: wholeness was juxtaposed by brokenness. The Dreaming presented a primeval order in the light of which an unpredictable existence would make sense. The Murimbata, says Stanner (ibid., 70), express a "perennial good-with-suffering of order-with-tragedy." It is as though they "suck in the orderliness" of sign patterns (ibid.) to counterbalance the amorphous. ·

We must digress here for a minute to the study of religion in general. As the Murimbata's view of life is crucial for the interpretation of their religion, Stanner (ibid., vi) feels that religion should not be studied solely as the dependent variable to discern the effect in religion of some set of social or psychological variables; instead, it must be studied "as religion and not as a mirror of something else." He therefore accuses those who view totemism, or society, or power legitimation as the essence of religion of confusing the part with the whole (154-55). Myths, on the other hand, deal vividly and fully with the whole. "The stories of founding dramas . . . transformed the archetypal past into an ontological process in which every Now could be justified or judged by Then" (155).

Yet this did not mean that the beliefs to which people referred when an account had to be given were "at all well stitched together" (157). Neither society nor culture could be regarded as a unified system or an integrated whole. At the most, one could talk about "workings towards system and transient captures of unity" (165). Or, in our terms: the vision of the order represented by The Dreaming could only superficially alleviate the precariousness of the mundane. Yet dramatization of the difference between the vision and the mundane was a perpetual source of strength. The mythical dramatizations sacralized the intermeshing manifestations of The Dreaming, the clan, moiety, tribe, manhood, femalehood, and personhood.

Understandably, Eliade (1973, 196) regards Stanner as a valued comrade-in-arms in his crusade against anti-historical and reductionistic interpretations of religion which he detects in "sociologisms" and "psychologisms." He assumes that both his own and Stanner's approach avoid the sin of reductionism.

This is manifestly false. Taking religion seriously as a *sui generis* phenomenon is no guarantee of anything. Any scientific study of religion reduces religion to a phenomenon to be observed rather than celebrated. Only in the latter instance is it *not* reduced. One creates a false dichotomy (remarkably prevalent amongst scholars of religion) if one defines the phenomenological, historical approach to religion as non-reductionistic (and therefore more true) and the anthropological/psychological/sociological approach as committing the sin of reductionism.

Yet it is true that it is less than scientific to explain religions away as nothing but "primitive science," "a collective neurosis," or "social solidarity." But this does not mean that scholars of religion can avoid thinking deeply and comprehensively of the interdependence of religion and other structures (historical, social, cultural, and psychic). Considering interdependence is tantamount to studying an effect (religion as the independent variable) and a being affected (religion as the dependent variable). And this, by implication, takes away from religion's exalted, *sui generis* nature.

Our topic at hand, the interaction between order and disorder in Aboriginal myths, shows awareness of the interdependence of sacred and profane phenomena. The Aranda myths of origin are essentially about the dialectic between order and disorder. What do they say?

To the Aranda (Strehlow, 1964, 725) the sky is inhabited by a emu-footed Great Father (Kngaritja) who had dog-footed wives and many sons and daughters. All the males are emu-footed and all the females dog-footed. In other words, the earthly totemic divisions between males and females are reflected in the order of the sky-beings. Or the other way round: the sky order is a paradigm for the divisions of the mundane. Yet, the sky-world does not have any of the normal features which break order down: the land is green and there are no droughts. The Milky Way flows through this land like a broad river, the stars alongside it are the campfires of the sky-dwellers. The latter are ageless. Death, disorder par excellence, does not exist in the sky-world. It would not have existed on earth either, had it not been for the breaking of the ladders connecting earth and sky.

Yet the separation between the order of the sky-world and the cracked order of the earth is complete. The Great Father does not exert any influence, does not create the earth, and has no power over winds. Yet the paradigm of order relativizes the earth with its ever-lurking disorder. It thereby makes that mundane world manageable.

The sky-order, however, is by no means the only paradigm of order for the Aranda discussed in Strehlow's article. The sky-world may be a superimposition on an earlier tradition in which The Dreaming is central. According to this tradition the active formation of the earth and its inhabitants took place at The Dreaming. Originally the earth was a shapeless, desolate nothing. The Ancestral Beings sleep under this amorphous surface. Some of them have animal shapes, others are entirely human, and again others are half-human, half-animal. However, their shapes are rather irrelevant inasmuch as they change themselves at will.

They break through the surface of the earth and slice up massed humanity, separating individual from individual; they slit the webs between the fingers and toes of the half-developed embryos, which are lying around helplessly. They cut open ears, eyes, mouths (Strehlow, 1974, 727-28). They also teach humans how to make tools and cook food. Some of them become the sun, moon, and stars. Other ancestors become rocks, trees, or sacred objects (*churingas*). Again others become spirit-children, entering wombs to be born as humans.

There are many other myths about The Dreaming, always closely related to a specific landscape. In North-Western Australia, for instance, The Dreaming is called Lalaininge. Here, too, the earth was originally lifeless and shapeless, a void. However, here Ungud, the creative power coming from below the surface, and Wallangand (Lord of the sky) co-operate. The latter threw drinking water down, so that life could begin. Creation is self-perpetuating, as Ungud (who is now bisexual) continues to live under the earth where a male and female Ungud snake are coupling, producing spirit-children endlessly (Lommel, 1969, 156).

3. Morality

The forms of order established at The Dreaming include morality. The Walbiri (Centre of the Northern Territory) think of the ancestors as dreaming forms which subsequently acquire more concrete shape (Munn, 1970, 145). To them and their neighbours, the Pitjantjatjara, these determinate forms comprise also the "moral imperatives, the lawful behaviour patterns of mores" (ibid., 151).

In contrast with Western society, Aboriginal society does not view the relation between morality and religion as dialectic (Mol, 1976, 95). There may be opposition between the firm ancestral order and the potential moral disorder of man, but religion and morality are indistinguishable and slide indissolubly over into one another (Berndt, 1970b, 219). Supernatural penalties are visited as indiscriminately on those who perform the ceremonies sloppily as on those who tinker with the moral relationships of the community (Mountford, 1965, 14).

Punishment for a moral transgression is brought out in one of the myths recorded by Mountford (ibid., 30). Kilpuruna is a bachelor friend of Yurumu and his wife Narina. One day he finds Narina alone in the forest, where she is collecting food. He attempts to persuade her to have intercourse with him, but she refuses, because, as she says, her husband would not like it. Yet she finally gives in, but feels ashamed and tells her husband about the adultery. He punishes her, but does not take vengeance on Kilpuruna until they are both together in a tall tree searching for honey. Here Yurumu unexpectedly pushes his friend from a branch, watching him crash to the forest floor. Flattened out by his fall, Kilpuruna becomes the blanket lizard. After the event Narina changes herself into a white cockatoo, flying "from place to place calling mournfully for Kilpuruna; Yurumu, now the wedge-tailed eagle, searches eternally to find and destroy his wife's lover, the blanket lizard."

Berndt elaborates his point about the combined moral and territorial function of the dingari myths as follows:"Fear, jealousy, quarrelling, trickery, theft, treachery, seduction, injury, murder and immolation infiltrate the moral orientation. These immoral acts are ... wrong in the same way as are drought, accident, and so on: they too turn to tragedy and disaster; they too, are 'immoral'" (1970b, 234-35).

In our own terms this means that wholeness (whether social or physical) is constantly in jeopardy. Placing these forms of breakdown in a mythical setting alleviates their effect. Again the order of The Dreaming is juxtaposed with the disorder of the mundane and is actually made to participate in this disorder, analogous to St. Paul's exclamation: "Death is swallowed up in victory [through Christ's vicarious suffering and resurrection]. O death, where is thy victory? O, death, where is thy sting?" (1 Cor. 15:54). In other words, disorder can be rendered innocuous. Order wins out in the final resort.

Yet the myths dealing with the moral order present, as often as not, the ancestors as amoral, if not actually immoral. The message is not necessarily that the ancestral beings are above the law and that man is under it. This may be the case. Yet, just as commonly they convey the message, as mentioned before, that the imperfect state in which man finds himself has its origin in ancestral deeds.

There is another point to be made about the many myths containing strikingly immoral acts by the ancestral beings.

Myths record almost no cases of licit sexual intercourse with mutual agreement of both parties; where there is mutual agreement the relationship is usually illicit, either incestuous or adulterous, or during a period of sexual taboo for one or other party; or if it is licit, it consists of rape, or it takes place after a long chase and difficult subjugation of the female (White, 1975, 123).

Sometimes the woman is injured or killed, because the hero's penis is too long. At other times the woman's dogs bite off the hero's penis, which then leads an independent existence and becomes a star in the Orion constellation (ibid., 130).

There are many myths of this kind and their function is obviously not moral. The mundane order is actually far more "moral" than the depicted ancestral one. There is also much more mutilating and murdering of relatives in myths than in reality. In these instances myths do for social identity what dreams do for personal identity: they relive and re-order experiences by bringing repressed desires to the surface (Mol, 1976, 258). However much repression is necessary for the integrity of a community, expression of what is repressed is also essential, functioning analogously to the safety valve on a boiler. The mythical dialectic between repression and expression of powerful aggressive and sexual sentiments is likely to have its own benefits for social cohesion.

In addition, those who tell the myths in which bad things go unpunished will safeguard public morality by saying at the end that what has happened belongs only to The Dreaming (Tonkinson, 1978, 17).

4. Rebirth Myths

There is a group of Aboriginal myths which deals rather fully with the identity/change theme. They are the myths which accompany the initiation rituals discussed in the previous chapter. Rebirth, or the change from one identity to another through being butchered and remade or swallowed and regurgitated, is the central idea.

We have already mentioned the Daramulun myth in which the boys are cut up and reformed out of ashes into initiated men. The same theme of a new identity being forged out of the dead elements of an old one is contained in the Mutjingga myth of the Murimbata. Mutjingga or Karwadi, the Old Woman, is a grotesque figure, half-woman, half-snake. She is an ancestral being with great authority. She has shaped the existent forms. One day she agrees to look after children while the parents are looking for honey. She tells the children to bathe and then to settle down to sleep in the shade. One of the children is brought close by, ostensibly to inspect it for lice. Then she swallows not only this one, but the other nine children as well. When the parents discover that all the children have disappeared, they organize a hunt for Mutjingga. She has hidden herself in the riverbed. However, the people discover the muddy patch where she is hiding and settle down, waiting for her to come up. When she finally emerges, Left Hand pierces both her legs with his spear and Right Hand breaks the Old Woman's neck with his club. They see her belly moving, cut her open, and find the children, alive and well in her womb (Stanner, 1966, 39-43).

The Murngin have a myth which is similarly interlocked with initiation and similarly of great importance to the tribe. It is at the time of The Dreaming that two Wawilak sisters and their children start out on a journey toward the sea, naming the animals, plants, and clan territories as they go. They are both pregnant as a result of incest and copulate with men from the same moiety. In addition one of them pollutes the sacred clan waterhole where the great python, Yurlunggur, the Big Father, lives. He goes to investigate and causes a flood by raising himself out of the well. Then he swallows the women and children. After some time Yurlunggur stumbles and becomes sick; he regurgitates the two women and their children into an ants' nest. When the ants come out and bite them, they revive and jump up (Warner, 1964, 240-47).

To the East of the Murngin in North-East Arnhem Land the same myths abound, but the details vary. For instance, the snake Julunggul, "the headman of all the animals, birds and vegetables," is now female. Yet her entry into the hut where the Wawilak sisters are crouching "is like a penis going into a vagina." The whole process of subsequent swallowing of the sisters in this myth is interpreted as coitus (Berndt, 1951, 21-25).

The Walbiri (North-West of Alice Springs) put the myth accompanying the initiation ceremonies in a family setting. Two ancestors from The Dreaming have to leave their wives and many young sons because food has become scarce in the nearby region. But before they leave they circumcise their sons, who are approaching puberty. The wives are very angry because of the cavalier way in which the men treat the sons; also, they feel excluded. After the men have flown away, the women kill their sons, eat them, and hide themselves in a cave. On their return the husbands track them down through the flies streaming into the cave and into the gaping, blood-stained mouths of the demonic women. The brothers then burn the women to death. But now they have neither sons nor wives who can provide them with children. Through a dream, however, they learn how to perform the ritual of the budgerigar parrots. During the performance the ghosts of the murdered sons appear in the trees and then several re-animated youths come on the scene. The ritual of the parrot song is repeated until scores of boys crowd the clearing (Meggitt, 1966, 55-59).

Although the details of the myths vary, the common theme is clear. Like the rituals of the previous chapters, the myths essentially deal with the transition from one phase (separation, swallowing, being killed) to another phase (being revived, regurgitated, re-animated) via a transitional period of resting inside the sky-being, python, or demonic women. A new wholeness results from the breakdown of an old one. The sex or form of the swallower varies as much as the sex or age of the swallowed. Nor does it seem to matter very much whether the swallowed disappear in the womb or the stomach, despite psychoanalytical insistence that the uterus is central to the explanation. The variety here is as great as the variety we found in initiation procedures or burial practices. The myths, then, mediate (or make the transition plausible) between two opposing delineated identities, boyhood and adulthood.

One of the myths, that of the Murngins, contains a closely interwoven subsidiary theme about which there is some controversy. Nature, which to Aboriginals is so indissolubly interwoven with social organization, has its own death and rebirth cycle in Northern Arnhem Land. The rainy season (Yurlunggur rising out of the waterhole and causing floods) alternates with the dry season (the Wawilak sisters are swallowed and Yurlunggur, the python, goes to rest). It is this unceasing alternation in the form of the Murngin myths which Lévi-Strauss, following Warner (1964, 385ff.), stresses: "the rainy season literally engulfs the dry season as men 'possess' women, and the initiated 'swallow up' the uninitiated, as famine destroys plenty" (Lévi-Strauss, 1966, 96).

But, reason Warner and Lévi-Strauss, if the dry (or good season, with rich social life) is represented by the females and the wet (or bad season, with famine and poor social life) by the males, the socially inferior and fertile element is being attributed to the masculine instead of the feminine. And this is a gross anomaly.

Warner (1964, 377) resolves the problem by saying that fertilization is more important than social superiority, which is therefore allowed not to fit into the myth, which he elsewhere describes as the categories to which the natives "refer their ideas and the things of this world in their ultimate meanings" (1964, 381). If, however, myths represent a self-consistent internal logic, as Warner assumes, then parts cannot very well be "non-fitting."

Lévi-Strauss (1966, 94) resolves the anomaly rather lamely by saying that the Murngin disguise the inconsistency "by the double division of the whole society into the two classes of men and women (now ritually as well as naturally differentiated) and the group of men into two classes of old and young, initiated and uninitiated . . . ." This I take to mean that the overlapping categories make a pure association of maleness and social superiority impossible. Then he washes his hands of the whole affair by noting (95) that "myths try to explain facts which are themselves not of a natural but a logical order . . . ." Further, he explains that "appeal must be made to form and not content." Yet both the "logical form" consistency and the "natural content" are at stake.

Understandably, Hiatt (1975a, 146) does not believe in the double division and does not think much of the solution of the anomaly. Yet he fails to solve it, apart from correctly pointing out that all the myths deal essentially with "charters for initiation ceremonies" and "contain the motif of swallowing and regurgitation" (155).

It may be that the anomaly can be solved by taking Lévi-Strauss's "bricolage" (the use of handy materials as conveyors of more essential symbols) in a content-related rather than form-related manner. In the actual myths the snake is now male, now female, or both together (Berndt and Berndt, 1977, 251 observe the same for the Rainbow Snake in other Arnhem Land myths). To say that the snake must be logically female because it represents fertility, or to say that it must be logically male because it has a phallic shape, upstages the general context of the myth at the expense of its message. In this particular myth femaleness may not represent fertility, as the carrier and the symbol are independent of one another. Exhaustive comprehension and logic should not be overestimated in any myth. Aesthetic representation and logical consistency are polar, as Lévi-Strauss should be the first to know, seeing that he admirably relates them both in his works.

However paradoxical this may sound, the crux of the matter is that one should not accord too salient a place to maleness and femaleness in a myth which deals with rebirth. Rebirth here relates to initiation into manhood and not to fertility. However salient femininity or masculinity may be in other myths, here they are obviously subsidiary themes, even to seasonal alternation, as in the Murngin myth. Here the carrier (gender) of the symbol is less relevant than the symbol (rebirth) in the heirarchy of meaning. In Lévi-Strauss's formulation of the problem the logic of the intermeshing part is too pivotal and the meaning hierarchy not pivotal enough. For the major theme to stand out, the minor elements may have to be manipulated and their logic reversed.

Warner and Lévi-Strauss are not the only major scholars who have concerned themselves with Arnhem Land rebirth myths. Mircea Eliade is another. He is very much aware of the death and resurrection theme in the initiation ceremonies, which theme, he says, "is widely known in the history of religions" (1973, 95). For him, as for Durkheim and Warner, these ceremonies and myths are essentially transitions from the profane to the sacred. The youths now become bearers of the secret sacred lore. Process is linear: from the profane to the sacred, not from the sacred to the sacred. The latter possibility does not fit into Eliade's scheme because it would destabilize the sacred as varying with its locus of attachment. There is no place for a desacralization of one identity and for sacralization of a new one. Identity and the sacred have to be kept in separate compartments, as identity is obviously subject to change, whereas the hallmark of the sacred is its inviolability.

Therefore, for Eliade, all the emphasis in initiation ceremonies is on the movement toward the sacred and not on the detachment from, or desacralization of, boyhood. The pervasive symbolism of death in both the rites and the myths consequently gets orphan status: it is not boyhood and attachment to the females which are central, but the profaneness of boyhood and femininity. And yet it is the dramatization of the opposing elements which makes the myth sacred, not the resurrection element alone as distinct from the death (or being-swallowed) element. Through this emphasis an important link with the vast amount of psychological literature of conversion is negated (Mol, 1976, 50ff.). Yet the death/profane and resurrection/sacred linkage to which Eliade's assumptions logically lead is absurd. Neither the rites nor the myths would carry this interpretation and therefore Eliade is wise enough to leave any logical linking of this kind alone.

5. Fire and Water

There is a group of Aboriginal myths in which fire plays a prominent part. As in many other cultures, some of these deal with its origin. Tribes in North-Western Australia trace it to two brothers, Kambi and Jitabidi, who lived near the Southern Cross in the sky. As food was getting scarce, they decide to come to earth. They go on a possum hunt, but leave their fire sticks behind. Now the sticks become rather bored with nothing to do and begin to chase one another, upon which the grass catches fire. The brothers return at once, gather the fire sticks, and journey back to the sky. However, a group of Aboriginal hunters takes advantage of the fire and takes a blazing log back to its camp. And since that time Aborigines have possessed fire (Mountford, 1965, 22).

An altogether different version of the origin of fire comes from South-East Queensland. On the advice of an ancestral being, certain natives go to the area where the sun comes out of a hole in the morning and where it disappears in another at night. Rushing after the sun they manage to knock off a piece and in this way obtain fire (Howitt, 1904, 432).

Sharing of fire is the motif of other myths, one of which belongs to natives in the Melbourne area. Karakarook (a woman of the Pleiades or Seven Stars) is the only possessor of fire. She keeps it in the end of her yam stick and refuses to share it. But Waung (the Crow) tricks her into killing snakes with the yam stick, upon which the fire falls out. Now Crow is the only one who can cook, but like Karakarook he refuses to share it. He will cook for the natives, on condition that they will let him have the best pieces of meat, and he is loath to surrender this obvious privilege. All this makes Bunjil, the sky-being very angry and he makes the natives speak very harshly to Waung. The latter then surrenders fire, but out of spite throws it amongst them. The natives pick it up and two of them burn Crow with it. However, they also burn themselves and can now be seen as two large stones at the foot of the Dandenong mountains. In addition, Bunjil punishes Crow by changing him from a man to a bird.

In other myths fire is contrasted with water. Stanner (1966, 32) mentions the Murimbata myth in which the eagle-hawk (one moiety) and the kite-hawk (the other moiety) are continually in conflict with one another. Each possesses a vital resource, fire or water, without which the other cannot live. Through learning to co-operate they are saved from death. This myth is a good example of the contribution a myth can make to the balance between conflict and co-operation of one identity (moiety) in the larger tribal context.

Hallam links fire and fertility, on the basis of cave paintings in various parts of Australia. Both fire and fertility are symbols of the

Fertility Mother. On the basis of her findings, Hallam then provides evidence for the general juxtaposition of blood/water/snake symbols for male potency and earth/fire/fertility for femaleness (1975, 96). Maddock (1970, 190) has also made a study of the Australian fire myths and similarly concludes that they contain a basic dialectical play between the compatibilities and incompatibilities of water and fire.

6. Conclusion

One can think about the myths we have examined as dealing with two contrasting modes. On the one hand they ceaselessly delineate. The territorial myths sharpen the boundary of clan and tribal identity. This identity, moreover, is reinforced by the givenness (its opposite, chaos, is always the enemy!) of the physical shapes within. The Dreaming delineates order. It thereby minimizes the unpredictable and maximizes the management of existence.

Yet this management can never do away with both predictable and unpredictable change. What is more, the very delineation of order can be a disadvantage for coping with change. There must also be a mechanism for making the outlines vaguer. Therefore, on the other hand, myths also deal with transitions, transformations, and the guiding of change, so that the latter does the least amount of damage to order. Yet all other myths dealing with the reconciliation of binary oppositions do the same. By making an allowance for opposition they can check, tame, and contain.

The excessive amount of sexual and other violence in Aboriginal myths is a means to contain by expression. The very real, antisocial forces in man's basic makeup are tamed in the very articulation of them, not dissimilar to the treatment of the absurd in the art and theatre of the absurd.

Yet more important are the kaleidoscopic and infinitely variable dramatizations of the wholeness/breakdown or identity/change theme. Myths narrate. Some of these narrations are simple tales. One of the problems with the literature on Aboriginal myths is that only the best scholars let the reader know how important and how sacred the myths are. Wherever discriminations were made between sacred and secular myths, the former always proved to deal with these two fundamental modes: delineation of crucial wholenesses and transitions between identities when change made these transitions necessary.

6

Breakdown and Native Revitalization

Sometimes change goes berserk, spills over the carefully maintained breakwaters and embankments, and creates utter chaos, ruining everything in its path. That is the way it was in Aboriginal society after 1788.

The chaos following European colonization of Australia could not be contained within the delineations of order. The carefully orchestrated nomadic existence came to naught. The finely attuned Aboriginal authority structure was washed away when hunting became unnecessary and stone-age weapons were rendered obsolete. Hitherto unknown diseases, such as tuberculosis and influenza, decimated the population. European settlement and native mortality began to correlate calamitously.

This was particularly true for the South and the South-East of Australia. Hardly any full-blooded Aborigines are left there. The half-castes inhabiting the slums around the major cities have forgotten their native languages and traditions, if they ever knew them.

In the arid inland, the North and the West, things were somewhat better. Yet here too in the nineteenth century punitive expeditions and indiscriminate shooting of native bands sometimes followed the spearing of cattle and sheep, the raiding of crops and stores. If settler, pearl-fisher, and native arrived at some form of accommodation, venereal disease (the Aboriginal was happy to lend his wife for a bottle of rum) and alcoholic excess followed the transactions.

If the settlements did not ruin the natives, the natives ruined themselves. Their curiosity and their fascination with Western consumer goods often got the better of them. Tribal territories were abandoned and new settlements arose around the pastoral, mission, and government stations. So many Aborigines became permanent hangers-on that only a few hundred out of 100,000 Aborigines are still nomadic in the old sense of the word. Many more, however, go on the occasional walk-about. The advantage of the many social benefits (child endowment, old age pension, unemployment benefits), the hand-outs of food, and the provision of shelter, financed by millions of dollars from Aboriginal Welfare, is too great to be surrendered.

The picture of racial genocide or suicide is primarily a nineteenth-century one. Yet even today examples can be found of basic identity patterns being exchanged for the pottage of sensual delight. When recently, in Wiluna, Western Australia, Aboriginals gained free and easy access to alcoholic beverages, ritual began to deteriorate. Sackett (1977, 93) mentions initiation ceremonies being scheduled for a particular weekend. However, instead of carrying out the ritual the men "decide there is ample time to go into town for a quick drink .... Once being in town, the prospect of the long walk back to the reserve and the coolness of the beer tempt the men to stay until it is (1) too late to begin the ritual and (2) they are too drunk to do so anyway."

Further to the North-West in Western Australia (another area which in the nineteenth century could escape the ravages of culture contact) the Aborigines of Fitzroy Crossing offer their sacred objects for sale to the Australian Government because money means more to them than religion. The possession of the *darugu* (sacred boards) is no longer end but means (Kolig, 1971, 108). In Pitjantjatjara society (Central Australia) weakened authority and diminishing dignity of the older men correlate with increasing juvenile delinquency and withdrawal from religious practice (Wallace, 1977a, 87-88).

The generational division affected the rate of change. Occasionally the wiser, older Aboriginals would become frightfully aware of the collapse of their identity, but then the carefully circumscribed fatalism of the nomad would re-assert itself and they would take things as they came. Rolling with the punches of the inevitable was after all the traditional way of solving problems. To meet change head-on had never worked. To fit with nature, rather than to master it, was the sacred prescription. That in this instance fatalism could be fatal for an entire way of life was beyond their comprehension. Their worldview had no place for this unpredictable danger. The Western concepts of time, distance, and number, the European views of manipulation, were foreign and could not even be visualized. Visualization might have improved predictability and subsequent motivation could have provided a measure of invulnerability. But as it was, vulnerability was complete.

Yet the younger, more impetuous Aborigines often welcomed the change. The social identity, so sacred to the older men, was confining to them. Elementary instincts of eating, drinking, mating had been contained within the iron-clad system. But the newer European options burst the system wide open. It became as irrelevant after the provision of the wider range of options as it had been stable before.

There was now an alternative to eking out an existence in the desert. Scrounging around the white man's station and eating the crumbs from his table was an easier way of filling one's stomach than to spear and skin a kangaroo. There was now also an alternative to the older men's monopolization of wives. The breakdown of marital arrangements, encouraged by the missions, meant monogamy and greater choice. Daisy Bates (1947, 107) writes that out of a thousand marriages she became acquainted with in Western Australia not one was regular.

And so the collapse of tribal and clan identity, detribalization, the altered values imposed by settlers, missionaries, and government officials were to many of the younger men a blessing in disguise.

Yet the blessing was not only disguised. It was also very mixed. Parasitism might be a preferable option to nomadism, but indignity was not superior to dignity. Even if the instincts won out over the spirit, it was still regrettable that one could not have one's cake and eat it too. And this meant that, after the collapse, those who survived would attempt to rescue what could be rescued, which was little enough. They would try to glue together the scattered pieces with many borrowed elements from a civilization which had acquired so much that it could happily share the surplus, whether tobacco, flour, or salvation.

Fortunately for the Australian Aboriginal, the building of a new identity or the restoration of an old one was made easier as time went on. A major aid was the crack in the white worldview which led to an enhanced appreciation of the wholeness of ethnic and other group identities. But before going into this, a more minor, demographic, factor should be mentioned.

In the same way as aging and dying without replacement undermine a race, so an increase in the birthrate can have both physical and immaterial consequences. This is exactly what has happened in recent decades with the Aboriginal population. Broom and Jones (1973, 70) estimate that presently the growth rate of the Aboriginal population for Australia as a whole is a very high 3.4% per annum. This estimate is based on a crude birthrate (1966-71) of 44 per 1,000 and a crude death rate of 10 per 1,000. On this basis they project a doubling of the Aboriginal population between 1966 and 1986 and a trebling by 1996. This means that the number of 96,632 Aborigines in Australia according to the 1966 census (the figures include those who are less than half-aboriginal) may rise to 195,452 in 1986 and 289,515 in 1996. And this physical revitalization has inevitable consequences for a social resurgence.

The opportunities for ethnic consolidation changed for the better in the third quarter of the twentieth century. Nowadays preservation of different cultures is encouraged rather than discouraged. It is one of the ways that society at large unburdens its guilt about a hitherto unconscious and therefore all the more ruthless insistence on assimilation to Western ways. As these Western ways provide an increasingly less stable frame of reference, nostalgia for an imaginary, stable past increases. And with this nostalgia goes a hankering for preservation, whether of a threatened species, native customs, or the old wood stove. Gathering antiques and staging corroborees for tourists have therefore become a profitable pastime. And however much romantic sentimentalism is a superficial treatment for much more basic problems (it is somewhat like applying band-aids to a broken leg), it has doubtless given new opportunities for embattled foreign enclaves.

The basic problem, as indicated, is not an Australian problem. It is part of a worldwide realization that too much individualism and too much amorphousness of the larger social structure may be counterbalanced by shoring up endangered group identities. This is particularly true for countries of immigration with many ethnic enclaves. It is less true for countries such as Yugoslavia which have long suffered from too much ethnic awareness.

The main point so far has been that a problem in Western society (its amorphousness) can be turned into an advantage for those groups which are intent on repairing their battered and bruised integrity. What forms does this regeneration take in Aboriginal society in Australia? There are at least four (native, missionary, sectarian, and secular), and we will take each in turn. The first we will discuss in this chapter, the other three in a separate chapter on the way Europeans affected revitalization.

1. Native Revitalization

A distinction should be made between those Aboriginal groups which have managed to keep most of their identity intact and those which have lost it almost altogether. The further North one goes, the more likely one is to meet the first category. And the further South, South-East, and South-West one goes, the more likely one is to find only a vague shadow of the original traditions.

The earliest native revitalization on record occurred at the beginning of this century. It was called the Kurangara cult. Petri (1954, 268) regards it as the reaction of younger Aboriginals to the increasing incapacity of their elders to come to terms with change brought about by the Europeans. They found in the strong magic of the Djanba spirits (very tall, skeleton-like spirits with long sexual organs) an inner support missing in the religion of their fathers. The Djanba are visible only to the initiates. They can see everything that is hidden and can kill at a distance.

Although the cult came from further East, the younger men of the West Kimberley tribes were attracted to it as a substitute for the very painful circumcision and subincision ceremonies (Petri, 1954, 262). Lommel (1969, 166) regards the Kurangara cult as an attempt to incorporate European civilization into the native one. It stresses the strange and the powerful as organically part of the tradition.

The Northern Territory is the most likely area in Australia for a successful native revitalization movement to occur. Here Aboriginals have retained more of their old traditions than elsewhere. In addition their recently acquired political and economic power (they have won their Land Rights litigations and may earn hundreds of millions of dollars in mining royalties) provides a strong base for a new, independent identity.

In a perceptive article Catherine Berndt traces the effect of World War II on the region. The Army settlements employed Aborigines from near and far. The Aborigines not only worked together with the soldiers, but egalitarianism extended also to the off-duty hours. Whites and blacks equally enjoyed the gambling and card playing "which almost paralysed [the base] for a few days after the fortnightly pay" (1961, 19).

Yet the natives also found time for their traditional ceremonies, which were then often watched by other tribes. They would explain to one another: "This is how we Larakia do it," "That's how those Majali do it." In addition, living together encouraged a considerable amount of intertribal interaction, hitherto absent. After the war the settlements were disbanded, but only a minority of Aboriginals returned to their tribal territories.

Presently the Aborigines balance white and black culture by assigning to each its own sphere of influence. Maddock, who did his fieldwork on the Beswick Reserve, describes these two spheres as "whitefellow law" and "blackfellow law." Huge areas now come under the first: marriage across tribal divisions, monogamy, free choice, work for pay, the frenzy of gambling, and language (English is the *lingua franca*).

Yet at the very time that tribal allegiance weakened and the older ritual activists died, the younger men began to reinforce "blackfellow law" with the result that the big ceremonies have been celebrated more regularly and often since about 1960 than in the 1940s or 1950s (Maddock, 1977, 26). And Maddock (24) claims that in spite of "the untidy jumble of bits from one culture and pieces from the other . . . the two laws are being grafted together."

Ceremonies may not take place on weekdays and pay weekends, yet they are being held regularly. There are all kinds of substitutions: kapok for feathers, cotton wool for wild cotton, margarine for animal fat, cardboard for paperbark, flour for pipeclay; yet consolidation of "blackfellow law" takes place around religion and it is on this religious level that pluralism gets its support.

Reconsolidation of native identity can also take other forms. A renewed interest in one's territory is the most obvious example. Here, too, very secular and very religious motives intertwine. In Arnhem Land dozens of small Aboriginal groups have moved away from the major settlements in order to be independent, to re-assert their link with the sacred country, and to have a stronger claim when prospecting and mining companies move in. The decentralization trends are strongly bolstered by the improvement of services and amenities which missions and government agencies can now provide to these outstations (Gray, 1977, 117).

Cynics should not overestimate the mercenary motives of the outstation movement. There are areas (such as the North-West of South Australia) where mining interests are minimal. Yet here, too, Aboriginals decentralize and have done so for quite some time (Wallace, 1977b, 124). The major motive here is the link with the tribal and clan heritage, and territory has been the traditional pivot for identity. A return is often instigated by lingering guilt-feelings about the neglect of the sacred places. On the other hand, without the supply lines of vehicles and stores, these guilt-feelings might have been permanently squashed.

Another motive for the return has been a vague feeling that dignity and authority might be restored if one moved away from the easy, but parasitic life around the missions, government, and pastoral settlements. The identity renewal is also, interestingly enough, accompanied by ritual. Wallace (ibid., 129ff.) describes how the sacred sites of these outstations are ritually approached by the placing of hands on the sacred objects. After this, newcomers are let to the site and an explanation is given of the objects and the ancestral spirits contained in them.

There are other Aboriginal attempts to rescue identity from the disorganization of culture contact. In the Fitzroy area of the Southern Kimberleys an influx of Desert tribes from the South took place in the first half of this century (Birdsell, 1970, 118). These tribes replaced the disastrously decimated native groups of the area. They absorbed the remnants of these tribes with a few interesting exceptions, about which more will be said later.

With respect to the Wolmadjeri (the predominant, desert-originated tribe), Kolig (1977, 39ff.) describes the forging of a new tribal identity, now enlarged with other remnants. The migration, he says, necessitated the extension of the boundaries between Aboriginal groups who considered themselves as belonging together (having a common sense of identity—*djandu*) in contrast with the groups which were regarded as alien (*ngai*). Contact made these lines more fluid. Still, greater fluidity was followed by a subsequent consolidation of new boundaries by means of linguistic and typically Desert-like religious ceremonies.

Yet this Wolmadjerization did not run smoothly. There was a marked boundary conflict with the surviving remnants of the Bunaba tribe, who retained their cultural independence and "did not accept Desert cultural background which they superstitiously fear as evil and dangerous, and at the same time despise as barbaric and crude" (ibid., 48).

Wolmadjerization is accompanied (or even encouraged?) by feelings of opposition to European society, which is regarded as discriminatory and oppressive. Consolidation of an all-Aboriginal identity stems from the "socio-political contrast vis-à-vis the unwanted dominance by racial aliens" (ibid., 49). Kolig sees this new all-Aboriginal identity as the final stage of the expanding traditional identity concepts. "Contrast is no longer experienced in intra-Aboriginal terms, but identity is found in contrast to another foe, the white man" (50).

The article provides little evidence for this "all-Aboriginal identity" and the ever-widening horizons of their meaning-system. Yet what appears to be a vast and fast jump from tribal territorial identity to twentieth-century racial consciousness is in actual fact well documented, as will be seen in the discussion of the Pindan mob described in the section on secular revitalization in the next chapter. This mob inhabits the same region.

Kolig defines social identity, not as *sui generis*, but as derivative of personal identity and a construction of the individual mind. This means that conflicts between personal and social identity or between social identities do not fit well in the frame of reference. Therefore "Aborigines do not experience identity problems because of ideational continuity" (ibid., 37), by which he means that the traditional ideological superstructure (The Dreaming?) has set the stage for an orderly sequence of changing identities. Yet having The Dreaming in common obviously did not solve the Wolmadjeri/Bunaba conflict. Nor is the sharpened conflict between Aboriginal and European identity congruent with a conceptual schema in which identities can only flow harmoniously into one another because they are constructions of the mind. Yet it is true, of course, that the absorption of remnants from other tribes by the Wolmadjeri was facilitated by similarity in worldview, and this is the brunt of Kolig's argument.

We must now turn to native revitalization in the more urbanized areas of Australia, where Aboriginal traditions are at the most a vague shadow of their former strength. Here, too, Aboriginal identity or "Aboriginality" has been on the upswing. Why would that happen when there is little upon which identity could possibly be built?

Let us first look at the literature on the subject. Donald Tugby (1973, 1) applies to Aboriginal society Cooley's concept of the looking-glass self (self-knowledge as reflected through the knowledge of others about the individual in question). Aborigines, he says, learned who they were from "a society of whites willing to provide a reflection: missionaries, frontiersmen, legal experts, administrators, and social scientists." Others in the book which Tugby edited put it even stronger. Wentworth (1973, 9) sees the Aboriginals exclusively as members of one tribe or, at the most, a group of tribes. "In a sense, the creation of an 'Aboriginal identity' is in itself a very un-Aboriginal process, for which there is no historical substructure." In the same volume von Sturmer (1973, 16) calls "Aboriginality a fiction which takes on meaning only in terms of white ethnocentrism." And further on he says that Aboriginal identity is "a concept that has only value as a political expedient" (ibid., 25).

Assuming then that the concept as such is a European reflection, or a historical anachronism, or fiction, why has the "fiction" taken hold of the part-Aboriginals?

The development of a supratribal Aboriginal identity is particularly visible amongst the part-Aboriginals' settlements around the Australian capitals. Inglis (1964, 115) speaks of the group-consciousness of the natives who never grew up in a tribal society on the Point Pearce and Point McLeay reserves near Adelaide.

Diane Barwick (1964, 20) describes the group-identity of part-Aborigines in the Melbourne area who were detribalized long ago.

John Wilson (1970, 81) discusses the part-Aborigine community of Cooraradale on the outskirts of Perth. Here too tribal origins and knowledge of Aboriginal traditions were less relevant than being a *nunga* (a term used to refer to Aborigines of the South-West of Western Australia) as opposed to whites who were termed *wadjalas*.

James Bell (1964, 64-65) writes about the absence of a traditional culture amongst the New South Wales part-Aborigines and yet points out the outspoken ethnocentricity of some of their communities. He draws the attention to the frauds or "professional" Aborigines who possess little knowledge of the traditions but make claims in order to impress the gullible white man.

Robert McKeich (1977, 262) discusses a survey he did amongst part-Aboriginal high school students. It shows how Europeanized their values are but how, on the other hand, they very much prefer the company of other part-Aborigines. He has a good bibliography of other studies of this kind.

The theme of Aboriginality versus Europeanism is also raised in Eckermann's work about a Queensland government settlement and urban community. Her anthropological participant observations are complemented by survey findings. They show that the Aborigines operate in terms of such European values as self-reliance and personal initiative. She even finds her respondents over-estimating and over-identifying with European values with the exception that they think of themselves as "black" versus "white," thereby welding themselves into an effective group (1973, 39-40).

However, in contrast with the others, she has evidence of a variety of Aboriginal traditions. For instance, in one of her kinship groups at a particular spring near Gayndah where the spirits of the old people are thought to live she found a common belief in *gundil* (anything possessing magical power, 1977, 303) or the baptism of children between the age of two and three years. All her part-Aboriginals also believe in *janjardi*, a little knee-high, hairy man, who is a friend of children. He will comfort them, but he may also run off with them into the spirit world. There is an equally widespread belief "in ghosts and in the return of the dead to visit their relatives" (ibid., 306-307).

Except in the last instance, traditional Aboriginal religion has no binding force. Yet the communities are held together by common family ties or sometimes a common commitment over against the white society. Aboriginality is for them a useful tool to accentuate their differences from others. By implication this reinforces their internal unity. As some of the above authors mention, there is very little difference between the Aboriginal communities and other ethnic European enclaves in the Australian cities. These observations may provide us with the clue to the Aboriginal group-consciousness: to have identity, even if it is built on a non-existent tradition, is better than to be lost in the formless wilds of the modern city. There is greater dignity in being an Aboriginal slum dweller and in belonging to a group of like-minded people of roughly the same skin colour than in being nothing at all.

Yet this kind of Aboriginal identity contrasts sharply with the groups in the North and North-West for whom The Dreaming, the sacred territory, and the totemic rites are the basis for a revitalized identity.

7

The European Effect on Revitalization

The reconstitution of Aboriginal identity could not fail to take over elements from the very civilization which destroyed it. The conquered had to come to terms with the conquerors if they were to survive at all. They borrowed bits, rejected others, and were greatly aided by the steadily increasing twentieth-century freedom to bring their own house in order. Here we will consider the missionary, sectarian, and secular elements which were built into the new identity.

1. The Missionary Effect

The missions amongst Aborigines in Australia are generally established by the major denominations: Anglican, Catholic, Lutheran, Methodist, Presbyterian, and, since 1977, the Uniting Church.

The major denominations can be distinguished from the sectarian groups in the next section through their traditional concern with the existing identity of their memberships. The latter groups are more likely to stress the creation of a new identity.

For our purposes this distinction is important, as the general tenor of denominations at large will be reflected in the mission field. The sectarian groups stand over against society at large. To them that society is close to perdition and they see it as their task to save a remnant from that perdition. The denominations, on the other hand, are more likely to stress the saving of that society. They are concerned with strengthening God's order in that society, whether through social action or through explicating meaning.

Christianity arose in conjunction with Western civilization. One can hardly think about the one without the other. Christianity represents Western thinking and acting. If lately the two are thought to be divorced, a less superficial analysis will soon reveal an essential congruence. Certainly the Aborigines thought and think about the two as very much belonging together.

Students of Aboriginal society often hardly conceal their impatience with the missions. A conflict of perspectives lies at the base of this impatience. The scholars of Aboriginal society attempt to understand that society from within, as a functioning whole. They have a stake in seeing it as an operating unit. To them the missions introduce a jarring element from the outside which interferes with what holds this society together, often precariously. They see a further destruction of the already tottering system of meaning which they think should be preserved.

Sometimes, however, this impatience represents a scholarly lack of realism about the inevitability and depth of the clash between cultures. This clash is always brutal. Being on the side of the threatened culture does not make it any less so. And in actual fact the missions to the Australian Aborigines have generally represented Western civilization in its most appealing, decent, and humane form, in contrast with those who exploited the natives for monetary or sensual gain.

Yet the mission represented Western civilization. And here lies the crux of the problem. They may have been in the forefront of learning Aboriginal culture and understanding Aboriginal customs, but in the final resort this was done in order to be more effective in bridging the gap, so that the Christian view could penetrate.

It is not sufficiently realized that the reinforcing of Western culture by the missions follows intrinsically the same path as the reinforcing of Aboriginal culture by The Dreaming and totemism. It is not particularly realistic to assume that the one is less necessary than the other, even though fairness requires one to be on the side of the underdog. It is utopian to think that contact between societies can leave both unperturbed, as though cultures are antiques to be preserved at any price. A strongly protected, hot-house culture is often doomed precisely because embattlement has its own preserving consequences.

Yet this does not mean that the Australian missions to the Aborigines have been as astute as they could have been. The late Father Worms of the Pallotine mission in North-West Australia, himself a noted anthropologist, insists in an article (1970, 374) that missionaries must have a fundamental anthropological and linguistic knowledge. He feels that the missionary can avoid feeling lost in strange surroundings only when he is armed with that knowledge. Still, knowledge in itself is often not sufficient. The effect of the Apostolic Mission at Jigalong (minimal though it was) was greatest when the missionary had a good rapport and was genuinely liked (Tonkinson, 1977, 69).

It is not just the training of missionaries which is at fault. Often the comparative knowledge to improve the training hardly exists. Only now does it begin to dawn that there are fundamental similarities between The Dreaming and salvation (whole-making), or between the "crackedness' of existence and the Fall. Or that all religions, however primitive or advanced, address themselves to the problems of order. Unremitting faith in the *churingas* and undying commitment to the Lord Jesus Christ have similar, identity-preserving characteristics. The stripping away and welding of the initiation ceremonies are structually very similar to Christian conversion, however more voluntary the latter may be. The fact that Aboriginal myths are orally transmitted and that Christian beliefs are embedded in the literary tradition is less important than that both fundamentally deal with reconciling existential oppositions, whether order/disorder, femaleness/maleness, wholeness/breakdown, or salvation/sin.

Yet all these similarities cannot do away with fundamental differences. Specific views of individual/society relations, of marriage and family, of moral and immoral behaviour, are seamlessly interwoven with religion and culture. In one of the very oldest and most respected of Aboriginal missions in Australia (Hermannsburg in Central Australia, begun in 1877 by the Lutherans), which C.T.F. Strehlow supervised for twenty-eight years and where his son, professor of anthropology T. G. H. Strehlow, was born, a Western, Christian sense of community proved to be incompatible with Aboriginal and clan identity in the 1970s. The situation is now on the mend. Although one has to be careful with the assumption that Aboriginal identity will be restored automatically, provided that it is allowed to find its own level, Sommerlad's linking (1973, 67) of Western paternalism and Aboriginal anomie has a grain of truth in it.

The contribution of the Christian mission to the creation of a new Aboriginal identity has not been great. There is ample evidence that the many Christian baptisms, confirmations, marriages, and funerals were, for the Aborigines, ways to dutifully meet Western expectations (and Aborigines were masters of obsequiousness) without much effect on identity and motivation.

Daisy Bates humorously relates the story of the visit of Bishop Gibney of Western Australia to the Spanish Trappist monastery at Beagle Bay (near Broome) in 1900. Knowing that he was not likely to visit the mission again, the Bishop decided to have a confirmation service for the natives. Arraigned in his splendid robes of lace and purple and mitre he annointed sixty-five wild men and women and babies with oil in the little bark chapel, and gave them the papal blessing and the little blow of the "*Pax tecum*" on the cheek. Later Bates (1947, 15) visited the newly-confirmed Christians in their camp. She continues:

Imagine my mingled horror and delight to find Goodowel, one of the corroboree comedians, sitting on a tree-trunk with a red-ochred bill-can on his head, and a tattered and filthy old rug around his shoulders. In front of him pranced every member of the tribe, all in a line, and each wearing a wreath and veil that were a bit of twisted paperbark and a fragment of somebody's discarded shirt. As they passed Goodowel, each received a sounding smack under the ear with a shout of "Bag take um!" Hilarious and ear-piercing shrieks of laughter followed each sally. I went back in glee to tell the Bishop. He shook his head. "Ah, the poor craytures!" was all he said.

This lack of seriousness is, of course, not typical. Yet the shallow impact of Christianity on traditional acting and reacting is typical, even while the native identity is dissolving right before the natives' eyes.

Yet, however little the missions may have affected native identity and motivation, "had it not been for the work of Christian missionaries, it is doubtful whether Australian Aborigines would have survived into the present" (Burridge, 1973, 207). The change brought about by some of the missions is not inconsiderable. Worms (1970, 377) lists, for instance, the learning of trades (carpentry, baking, plumbing, mechanics, and so forth) by the younger men. He also mentions (and this certainly changed Aboriginal identity in the area) the substitution of baptism and consecration for circumcision and subincision by means of the circumcision being carried out in the hospital. He also lists the establishment of monogamy and the abolition of child marriage. Under "setbacks" (ibid., 378) he lists ritual blood drinking when visiting the initiation ceremonies of neighbouring tribes, the eloping, the fierce fights, and the harsh treatment of women.

The Protestant missions followed a variety of policies, but their combined effect on the establishing of a new Aboriginal identity did not differ much from that of the Roman Catholic missions. The evangelical Anglican Church Missionary Society (C.M.S.), for instance at Angurugu, Oenpelli, Roper River, Groote Eylandt, and Numbulwar in the Northern Territory, originally followed a policy of

assimilation, which meant that it valued Aboriginal culture somewhat negatively and that it set out, as the common expression was,
"to smooth the pillow of a dying race." It did this by protecting the
Aborigines from bush massacres, ill-treatment at the hand of the
pastoralists, and the urban vices.

More recently (Cole, 1977, 197-98), the C.M.S. had begun to
follow a policy of self-determination for the natives. Aboriginal beliefs are now seen as preparatory to Christian views of creation, life,
fertility, and the land. It is now less convinced about the dying of the
race and thinks that the real threat to Aboriginal traditions comes
from the "growing materialism and the clamour for motor vehicles,
transistors, tape recorders, alcohol and Western films" (ibid., 197).

The Methodist Overseas Mission has from the beginning followed a policy of respect for local traditions. In contrast to the
C.M.S., for instance, it has taken the stand that "the Aborigines'
names are not only attractive and pleasant to the ear, but are also
treasured possessions" (C. Berndt, 1961, 26). Yet they have not been
any more successful in influencing the formation of a new Aboriginal identity. On the Yirkalla mission (North-East Arnhem Land)
where the Watermans did their fieldwork in the early fifties, both
conversion to Christianity and to agricultural modes of production
were unsuccessful. There were no converts from the beginning of
the mission in 1939 until 1953, even though the Aboriginals attended
church and showed great interest in Old Testament stories about
bloody massacres and New Testament miracles (Waterman and
Waterman, 1970, 105). Yet they happily adopted all the material
provisions, such as corrugated iron, knives, safety razors, toilet
soap, foodstuffs, and so forth. The interpreter of the mission services, who had high status in the community, also used Western-
type communal meetings to discuss clan affairs and ceremonies.
Yet the Aborigines resisted any change which involved their values
and their worldview (ibid., 109).

There are a number of reasons for the shallow impact of the
Christian mission. On the Aboriginal side, the transition from their
traditional beliefs to Christian beliefs is too great. To accomplish a
transition, channels for strong emotional redirection and vital re-
orientation must be opened up. Aboriginal society never developed
tasks of this scope.

Probably more important was and is the solid entrenchment of
initiates in the traditional religion. Between the generations there
may be much conflict about initiation, such as Long, for instance,
mentions for the Haast Bluff area. Yet those Aborigines that do not
submit will be outcasts (even on some mission stations) or figures of
fun among their own people for the rest of their days (Long, 1970,

327). Young men may respect the missionaries, yet their allegiance is to their fathers and the secret life (Elkin, 1974, 188). Therefore missionaries of long experience complain that "boys are far less teachable ... after passing through the ceremonies" (Stanner, 1966, 19).

However, this also means that, in those areas at least, one cannot speak about an "identity destruction." Identity here is strong enough to resist the whites on whom the natives otherwise depend for their material comforts. It is more serious for the missions that their impact has been equally shallow where Aboriginal identity was destroyed, as obviously here the mission variety of Christianity was not a live option.

On the missionary side, the established Christian denominations train their personnel to maintain, consolidate, and purify the existing Christian tradition and identity. Here the channels that prepare for strong emotional redirection and vital re-orientation were available in the tradition, but were clogged up, as they always are when the task at hand is maintenance of the within rather than absorption of the without.

2.   The Sectarian Effect

There is an amusing story of professor Baldwin Spencer's visit to the Hermannsburg mission in 1923. At the instigation of the Federal government he was to investigate the Aboriginal problem in the area (Central Australia) and to make recommendations for an Aboriginal training centre. In his report he made the unflattering suggestion that the mission should be abolished (Lohe, 1977, 345). "If the Mission were closed down to-morrow, not a trace would be left, apart from the buildings, of its previous existence and influence on the Natives. Those of the latter who belonged to it, would simply return to their old method of living, though perhaps rather less than able to support themselves in the bush than if they had not been accustomed to regular meals provided for them."

This was not all. Heaping insult upon insult, he further suggested that another denomination should take over: "In view of the complete religious, social, and industrial organization of the Salvation Army, and of the nature of its works and methods, I am convinced that work amongst the Aboriginals could be carried out more successfully by this than by any other body...."

Nothing came of this, as the Salvation Army was not interested and the Lutherans were happy to continue in spite of the rudeness suffered at the hand of a Melbourne anthropologist. Yet the point was clear. The Christian capacity for solving Aboriginal problems is variable. Spencer was ostensibly only interested in training schemes and the management of the care for half-castes, outcasts, the infirm, and the old. But there was a deeper point. He also mentioned the "religious" relevance of the Salvation Army. On the grounds of what we now know about the effects of charismatic movements on the Maoris in New Zealand and on Indian tribes in North America in the nineteenth century we may go a bit further than Spencer did.

Effective transition from an obsolete to a new identity is not likely to take place by means of propaganda for Western culture alone, whether by missionaries preaching Christianity or by secular militants fighting paternalism and exploitation with visions of proletarian solidarity and economic aid.

The Salvation Army in its early beginnings was the organization which had solid experience with this transition. It indeed preached conversion, but did not leave it at that. It left no stone unturned to lift the disprivileged out of the trough of despair and the fount of lethargy. It guided the transition with the utmost care, as it was unshakingly convinced that the specific outcast they were dealing with had it in him to be saved by, and washed in, the blood of the lamb. This would make this specific individual an altogether new human being.

The similarity with the potential in-laws carefully guiding the initiand, encrusted with their own dried blood, is clear. Whole-making in the sense of creating a new whole was hard work requiring total concentration and dedication. It was emotionally draining and yet ultimately it led to the supreme reward. After all the impossible salvation was actually wrenched from the impossible through God's grace. And it was God's grace which made the impossible transition possible and transparent for all to see. Again the image of the now shining, clean, and freshly washed initiate appearing for his mother as a new being, a real man, comes to mind as a suitable analogue.

Strangely enough, the story of the Salvation Army's disinterest is also typical of the Australian situation. In contrast with the charismatic success of sectarians amongst the disprivileged in many other nations, the incidences of sectarian effect on the formation of a new Aboriginal identity are few indeed.

These few, however, should be mentioned. Sectarian forms of Christianity have legitimately laid claim on the self-purifying, prophetic strain of the tradition. The revitalizing force is built into its theology and outreach. It is never satisfied with a shallow congruence between God's order and man's imitation of it. It therefore has the ready potential for protecting outcasts with the left hand against the conformity requirements of a culture which it reinforces with the right hand. If this incongruity appears too much, it must be remembered that the very uplifting of the disprivileged in the final resort prevents a more serious rupture of the social fabric later.

The main example of sectarian reinforcement of a new Aboriginal identity comes from Malcolm Calley's article on Pentecostalism among the Bandjalang (1964, 48ff.).

The Bandjalang tribe is situated in the extreme North-East of New South Wales where it meets the Queensland border. Its members are almost all part-Aboriginal and live on six isolated stations and reserves. They were first evangelized by the United Aborigines Mission, an evangelical, interdenominational body which regarded Aboriginal beliefs as doctrines of the devil. In 1952 the Mission was left in the hands of an ordained Aboriginal pastor on the Cubawee Reserve (near Lismore) and an unordained leader at Woodenbong (on the Queensland border). On a third reserve (Tambulan) a Pentecostalist evangelist who had lived and worked in a Sydney slum during the war took over. Soon his leadership was also accepted in the other settlements.

Pentecostalism was attractive to the Aborigines because it emphasized initiation in stages, as in its own heritage. First comes baptism in water (immersion) and then baptism in the Spirit. Individual magical power and healing rites were also similar to both. In addition Pentecostalism offered the consolidation of anti-white sentiments. The Bandjalang compare the whites with the Roman soldiers who crucified Christ and are therefore destined for hell. They, on the other hand, are like Christ, humble and poor, and therefore destined for heaven. "Christ is about to come back 'in glory' to reverse the social order and reward His pentecostal followers ..." (Calley, 1964, 52).

Indigenous mythology is intertwined with biblical teachings. The landing of the culture hero Ngathunggali (or God the Father) on the coast is explained as proof that they are among the "lost" tribes of Israel. Another hero, Balugan, is identified with Christ, and Gaungan with an angel or Mary. Balugan was killed and "every year Gaungan, appearing in bird-form dances the death corroboree for her son on Arakoon race course near Kempsey, where a large oblong stone is believed to mark the site of Balugan's grave ..." (ibid., 53).

Bandjalangs are very strict. They do not smoke or drink, attend cinemas or dances, or play music, except hymns. The sexual taboos on adultery are somewhat less strong than is normal in Pentecostalism and more akin to Aboriginal custom. On the other hand, the strong Aboriginal insistence on male initiation has been replaced by baptism of either sex. Women take an important place in the ceremonies, although Pentecostalism was introduced by the men, who are also the leaders and healers. Their religious status, says Calley, is often the only important status the men have. It is from Pentecostalism that the Bandjalang receive a new identity and social solidarity.

So far Malcolm Calley. It is interesting to see how the Bandjalang have fared since his 1952 fieldwork. In July 1978 I had an opportunity to spend two days in the Bandjalang district. Although the observations can only be cursory, it seems clear that the erstwhile Pentecostalism of the Bandjalang is in a rather precarious state. Only a minority practice their religion. Teachers, bank managers, Aboriginal religious leaders are unimpressed with the economic and other effects of religion. In the Woodenbong area hardly any of the Aborigines were employed and alcoholism was regarded as a grave problem, in spite of the fact that the Pentecostal leaders made non-drinking one of the major criteria of being within the fold. Insofar as Pentecostalism has survived since Calley did his research, it functions as a justifier for Bandjalang withdrawal from Australian society rather than as a catalyst for the pursuit of Western economic goals.

Yet the opposite is true for the Torres Strait Islanders who have migrated further to the South in Queensland. In the Pentecostal church in Bowen (the Church of God) the majority of participants in a church service which I attended were black. They did some of the preaching and all of the playing (guitars, drums, pianos, organ). None of them was unemployed and here Pentecostalism functioned clearly as a catalyst for the adoption of Western economic values.

This is also true for the Torres Strait Islanders who have become members of the Universal World Church in Townsville. Virtually all of the Islanders have joined this church, which provides the individual "with a larger and meaningful group into which he is received and which gives him a sense of 'belonging' that again greatly mitigates the effects of his alienation from the traditional island society he has left behind" (Fisk, 1975, 89). The Islanders refrain from smoking and drinking, which has enhanced their local reputation as reliable workers. Fisk observes that this is all the more remarkable as "the Islanders in Torres Strait itself are more often than not sturdy, if cheerful drinkers when the occasion permits" (ibid.).

The protest element in Christianity has also been appropriate in other areas of the continent. It happened around July 1963 that Jinimin (Jesus Christ) revealed himself to the Woneiga tribe (Central Australia) while they were singing about the dramatic female creators of The Dreaming (Petri and Petri-Odermann, 1970, 258ff.).

He was both black and white and proclaimed that all the land from the beginning belonged to the Aborigines and that all would equally share in the land. Jinimin revealed himself as protector and pre-server of The Dreaming. The Petris observe that the Jinimin ritual strongly contributes "to Aboriginal self-confidence and self-identification, providing them with courage and the inner strength to cope with the future and the changing (and in their view better) social order" (ibid., 259). The movement is strongly anti-white and has been influenced by ill-feeling over the establishment of the missile base at Talgarno. The ideas of Don McLeod (about whom more will be said in the next section) have also fed the anti-white stance.

By 1966 the Jinimin myth had spread to the West and was accepted by the Walmadjeri on the Fitzroy river. A chief prophet there was a medicine man and stockboy, Tommy Djilamanga. The Petris call him a charismatic leader, whose "name was on every lip" (260). Jinimin expressly ordered the return of ancestral beings of The Dreaming to their original territories. "They march on the underground routes, using camels which carry the belongings" (ibid., 263). Amongst these belongings are the *darugu*, cult objects which we discussed in a previous chapter.

Another influential leader and prophet of the Jinimin movement is Lulidj, a Walmadjeri at Fitzroy Crossing, "who identifies himself with the patriarch Noah and is said to have at his disposal an ark filled with crystal and gold" (265). This ark was sent directly from heaven to him by Jinimin, the preserver of the old Law of The Dreaming. According to the Aboriginal Bible kept in Myroodah station, the ark is a refuge for those loyal to the Law after the destruction of Europeans and after the Flood, which presumably will carry out this destruction. Yet the ark is also "the basis of the wealth of a future and more powerful Aboriginal society" (ibid.). The movement here also believes the personal witness of an Aboriginal who saw deceased Aborigines at certain mission stations rise from the dead after three days and ascend into heaven.

The cult rituals accompanying these syncretistic cults sharply differ from the traditional ones. Penalties are given for late arrival or early departure, scorning God's law, or embarking on an illegal marriage. The form of punishment for these transgressions consists in standing "for a whole day, from sunrise to sunset, under supervision in a shadowless place with hands raised and without food or water" (264).

While it is generally true that Christian sectarian movements are most likely to sound the anti-establishment note, this in itself does not guarantee their effect on Aboriginal society. Certain items from

Roman Catholic, Anglican, or Protestant preaching may be singled out by Aboriginals and form the basis of anti-white cults. And the other way round: messages from sectarian groups may have little or no effect.

Tonkinson gives a good example of the latter. Jigalong (in the Western Desert of Western Australia) used to be a station of the Apostolic Church Mission. It was started in 1946 and closed in 1969. It is now an experimental pastoral station. Tonkinson (1974, 119ff.) describes the emphasis of the mission on not smoking, drinking, swearing, gambling, sexual joking, and breaking the Sabbath as so strong that people who indulge in these vices are, by definition, non-Christian to the Aborigines. The missionaries had no specialized linguistic or anthropological skills to deal with Aboriginals. They tended to be ill at ease with the natives. They believed in baptism by the Holy Spirit and spoke in tongues (rather reminiscent of the Bandjalang Pentecostals), but they regarded the Aboriginals as corrupt, inherently evil, and steeped in sin.

To the Apostolic Mission, Aboriginal culture had to be completely destroyed before Christianity could have any effect. It was not the theology of the Apostolic Church, or even its asceticism, which made for conflict with the Aboriginals but its incapacity to anchor a potentially relevant message in the native tradition. The Church also lacked understanding of its own culture-bound base. The result of the avowed intention to destroy Aboriginal culture made the Aborigines all the more determined to maintain it.

The outline of an answer to our question as to what effect Christian sectarian movements had on Aboriginal reconstruction of a new identity begins to take shape. In the few areas where the effect has been recorded, selected messages about the inherent evil of society are woven into the anti-white belief system. The salvation of the remnant, also very much a biblical idea, strongly retraces the delineation around their weakened identity. Yet the greatest effect takes place where native charismatic leaders do the convicting and possess inexhaustible energy for guiding and healing "the broken-hearted." The combination of ancestral beings from The Dreaming and biblical theology is similarly typical for this kind of revitalization, as is the uncharacteristic (for Aborigines) adoption of stringent ascetic rules of behaviour.

3. The Secular Effect

In modern societies identities are sometimes structured around secular causes. These causes then acquire an awe-inspiring aura. Strong commitment is required of the insider and the commitments are reinforced by meetings, emotion-charged speeches, and action programmes. The cause itself becomes all-absorbing to the inner core. Converts to the cause are eagerly sought. Once they are part of the movement the converts derive a sense of belonging, identity, and purpose from the involvement.

A good example of a cause having this effect is provided by Clancy McKenna's observations when he helped Don McLeod organize a strike of Aboriginal pastoral workers in the Marble Bar area of Western Australia. McKenna, himself a half-Aborigine and raised in a traditional Aboriginal society, describes the scene as follows, through his interpreter, Kingsley Palmer (Palmer and McKenna, 1978, 87):

It was a big mob; complex, diverse, angry and afraid, determined to fight to the end and resist poverty and deprivation. This was no dying race. Clancy looked at the group, and felt a sense of pride swell up within him. This was a responsibility, and here was a purpose. Here at last was his home with his people.

While leading the group and working at a consensus, McKenna stresses the words "purpose," "direction," and "meaning." All these were formerly missing and now gave them and him heartwarming solidarity.

Don McLeod was a white man who had been contract boring for water in the area. He had extensive experience with the trade unions. He had been a member of the Communist party, but gave up his membership in 1947 out of disgust with the little support he received for his action among the Aborigines. In 1946, after listening to Aboriginal complaints, he organized a strike of 600 native stockmen against the exploitation by the station owners of the district. He and his helpers were jailed, yet the strike succeeded. Afterwards a native co-operative (Pindan) was formed which at first engaged in mining in the Pilbara. Later, in 1951, four large stations were bought. However, the co-operative went into liquidation and Don McLeod's mob went back to small-scale mining for tantalite, columbite, and beryl.

The "mob," as it is generally called, has its own set of ascetic rules, determined by consensus. In this way solidarity is assured. Violence has been ruled out. So has liquor. *De facto* relations are discouraged and there are many group pressures to conform. Punishment is meted out for being noisily drunk, being abusive, and disrupting the peace. The punishment consists of so many days of "hard labour" in the camp with a member of the committee as policeman (K. Wilson, 1970, 336).

Yet the cause itself now has less integrative power than the traditional rituals and corroborees, from which Don McLeod distances himself as being "caterwaulin" (Smith, 1971, 54). Yet the religious rites have become modernized. For instance, the group decided to have circumcision carried out in the local hospital. Katrin Wilson (1970, 344) describes the "mob" as having "a self-assertiveness and a self-reliance which is not found elsewhere among Natives in Western Australia."

Don McLeod's movement has had a strong regional impact on Aborigines. The Petris (1970, 255-56) note that his social progressivism gave wings to the fantasy of other Aborigines in the area. They mention as an example the Jigalong groups which have strong visions of an egalitarian society without any colour bar. They regard the Aboriginal leaders around Don McLeod as being responsible for the formation of "those anti-European attitudes and vague revivalistic-millenarian dreams which were current among some of these Desert Aborigines" (ibid., 257).

These visions have gained rather than lost ground over the last twenty years. Yet, in spite of the high regard in which Don McLeod is held by the natives in the Pilbara region, there is considerable tension between the Aboriginal groups affected by the movement, tension which is mainly caused by tribal differences and the anti-white policies. The "mob" is now split into several groups, one of which owns Strelley station where Don McLeod now lives (Tonkinson, 1977, 71-72).

One of the other causes which has given Aborigines a sense of identity has been the Land Right movement which began in 1966 and issued in legislation enacted in 1976 which gave to the Northern Territory Aborigines as freehold the land they held as tribal reserve. This land contains the uranium rich Arnhem Land. The legislation also gave Aboriginals the right to claim other traditional lands.

Like the Pindan co-operative movement, the Land Right movement also began with a strike. In 1966 Aboriginal stockmen at Wave Hill station in the Northern Territory walked off their jobs and set up camp near Daguragu on the station, close to a gorge with sacred totemic sites and paintings. Four full-blooded leaders of the Gurindji people to whom the sacred sites belonged wrote a letter to the Governor General of Australia claiming the tribal territory. Although the claim was denied, the letter was the beginning of the successful Land Right movement. The local cause was taken up by Aboriginals in other areas and gained the widespread support of academics, students, and the trade unions.

One of the fascinating aspects of both the Don McLeod and the Land Right movements is that the cause is, as such, less a religion to the Aborigines than it is to its white supporters. For the Aborigines the movements are not ends in themselves, but means to an inde-

pendent and religiously reinforced identity, for instance, the reten-
tion of the sacred ancestral sites. One has the impression that, in
public, the Aboriginals gratefully accept the indubitable and necessary support from efficient and dedicated and sometimes "professional" activists, but that privately they denigrate the white lack of
balance and "humbug." It certainly is true that many of the white
supporters of Aboriginal causes make the specific cause into a
militant religion. They are often alienated from, or certainly have
little understanding of, the religious basis of their own tradition.

Many examples can be found of the Aboriginal cause seemingly
functioning as an answer to the quest for white rather than black
identity. I will single out the example of Professor C. D. Rowley's
championing of the Aboriginal cause in his book *A Matter of Justice*
(1978). Rowley is the Director of the Academy of the Social Sciences
in Australia and Chairman of the Aboriginal Land Fund Commission. In his book he judges Christianity exclusively in terms of its
contribution to the justice issue. Its dogmatism (ibid., 159) is only
ethnocentric confusion. The Christian mission has been nothing
but a "partner of government and of business interest," a justifier of
"colonial expansion" (ibid., 158). If Christianity had done a better
job, "there might have been less brutal exploitation of Aboriginal
labour and less brutal means of extending the pastoral industry"
(ibid., 158-59). As for the Christian sects of largely Aboriginal con-
gregations, they foolishly project a deferred justice in heaven rather
than aim for one obtainable here and now on earth by political
means. Unless the Christian missions champion the matter of justice for Aboriginals, they sow the wrong kind of seed. And anach-
ronisms will be phased out of remote Australia (ibid., 174).

There is, of course, a grain of truth in most of this. And yet to
dismiss the meaning provision of Christianity as irrelevant compared with its capacity to solve particular political problems shows a
rather serious misunderstanding of Christian tradition. It may be
that human beings anywhere have always wanted to have a model of
order by which to measure and relativize the existing state of affairs.
And maybe that state of affairs was always "cracked" and "incomplete." The utopian drive for a quick perfection in the here and now
has usually floundered on the naiveté of the utopians. Worse is the
pathetic disillusion when a particular political or economic cause
has been won and the temporary sense of salvation is rapidly wearing off. It seems that Aboriginal hesitancy with abolutizing a cause at
the expense of The Dreaming is wiser than the rootless support of
white supporters who are under the illusion that identity and meaning can be won from specific social, political, or economic action.

8

Conclusion

This study is woven around the idea that wholeness and breakdown alternate in human affairs. Aboriginal society is therefore seen against the background of the dialectic between identity and change. The theme has been visible in all chapters, maybe too visible at times! Yet loyalty to a theme or a perspective is nothing new—nor is it particularly meritorious. The totemic principles of traditional Aboriginal society were an ordering perspective. And so were the systematic theories of the eminent anthropologists, historians, psychologists, and sociologists who studied it so diligently. More important than the loyalty to a perspective is what the perspective allows us to see. The proof of the pudding is not in the recipe, but in the result. What then did we see that might have otherwise escaped us?

Before the cyclone of European colonization shook it down as a house of cards, Aboriginal identity consisted of a precarious configuration of clan, moiety, tribe, manhood, femalehood, personhood. These were the major internal points of reference, all tied together in a specific territory which formed, as it were, the backdrop for all meaningful action. The territorial tie was as strong as the earth upon which it rested. And it was made even stronger by deep loyalty to The Dreaming, which pervaded all and ordered all. It, or better, the ancestors who personified The Dreaming, shaped what was shapeless and formed what was formless. They affirmed what was vague and delineated what had no boundaries.

Each of the totemic ceremonies delineated a specific identity. Yet the visually concretized Dreaming tied it all together in an indestructible order, which fitted the social relations as neatly as the waterhole and the mountain range fitted the landscape.

And yet the mundane was "cracked" in comparison with the whole in which it was reflected. Droughts and death, famine and sorcery, fights and jealousy, adultery and betrayal, illness and pain, recalcitrance and rebellion, all reared their ugly heads. And only some of these could be carefully tamed and unobtrusively channelled back into the familiar grooves. Yet the Aboriginals managed. The rebirth dramas and the powerful initiation rites stripped the spoiled brat of his puerile attachments and welded him into a responsible man. They did not make him into a leader of men, but they made him into someone on whom the weaker sex could lean rather than someone who leaned on it.

Even the terrors of death, the violence of murder, and the lurkings of passion could be warily managed by mythical articulations. Not that management left no loophole for further change and disorder. On the contrary, existence was never failproof. Disorder was only minimized under prevailing conditions. And even "prevailing conditions" were only a scant apology for weaknesses in the family structure, the exaltation of manhood, or undeveloped patterns of leadership.

And then the "prevailing conditions" did not prevail any longer. In the South-East of the continent the fury of the cyclone swept all the securities away until nothing stood erect. European colonization created entirely new options. Nature could be subdued and manipulated rather than revered and served. Europeans turned the tables around. They treated nature as though it were a female and a female as though she were nature. Ruthlessness and gentility were attached to the wrong objects in this upside-down world. Individual aggression was expressed rather than repressed. Conformity was relaxed and individual competition advanced. And in this upside-down world the sacred was devalued while achievement was valued. As though this madness were not enough, the mad were even allowed to rule the roost, appropriate the land, and uproot the sane. And the latter became parasites in their own land.

Wherever the white man settled in large numbers, the race lost its nerve and disappeared sooner or later, like a delicate plant which cannot survive the soot of the industrial city. Even in some of the sparsely settled areas disorganization was considerable, though disorder could be better contained.

Yet, whatever the degree of disorganization the wounds would have healed eventually, if death had not interfered first. Even where the breakdown was ostensibly complete, where the tribal traditions and languages were lost, where no full-bloods remained, native consciousness would re-assert itself in the part-Aboriginal communities. This was partly an attempt to rescue some dignity from outcast status in the urban slums. Yet it was also an astute response to new political opportunities in a pluralistic society where ethnic enclaves had become respectable.

Where the breakdown had been much more gradual, a compromise between white and black would begin to emerge. In the economic, political, and family-organizational sphere, white norms would prevail. Yet basic Aboriginal beliefs and rituals would be safeguarded from European encroachment and would form the essence of a separate identity. In some areas these two spheres are beginning to meld. Here and there a separate identity begins to be legitimated in terms of Christian social protest principles. Or time begins to be seen as having a decisive end and purpose. Cult solidarities begin to compete with tribal or clan solidarity. Particularly in the North, an independent economic and political base will give the Aboriginals the freedom to build up this new identity outside the white sphere of influence.

Yet the choice is contained within well-defined parameters. An exclusive Aboriginal revitalization is one of these choices. An unchanged, precontact framework of order, however, may not fit with present-day political and economic realities. On the other hand, the tendency amongst some of the whites to elevate these political and economic realities into selfconsistent belief systems has not been followed. Aboriginals may have been realistic enough to grasp the opportunities offered by strikes and Land Right legislation, but have been less prone than their white supporters to make specific causes into religious commitments.

The Australian Aborigine is no exception to the general rule that a breakdown of identity leads to social disorganization, alcoholism, delinquency, family disruption, and the like. The social cost of such a breakdown can be considerable. An increase in welfare payments of one sort or another follows an increase in social disorganization. Instead of being an asset to the economic life of a country, the uprooted person who has lost his bearings becomes a liability. He has to be rescued by society at large from complete destitution.

Yet the financial and institutional support which modern societies provide for the destitute does not solve the basic problem underlying the destitution. Financial support, prisons, homes for delinquents, meal provisions, hostels for alcoholics and for unmarried mothers, the entire apparatus of social work and psychiatric care, only touch the surface. They cannot remake a family or any other group identity. They cannot provide meaning and motivation where there was none before. They can only supply first-aid, administered in the hope that the problem will rectify itself. And as this does not happen, the welfare-bureaucracies deflect their impotence into self-serving adventures: further extension of services which only touch the surface of the problem and lead to impotence on a larger scale. And of course, they can always truthfully point out that without these services, things would be worse.

There is an additional problem. We have mentioned before how the Aborigine exchanged his dignity for the white man's handouts. This is true in a much more general way for the destitute or unemployed anywhere: one's self-respect and self-confidence (all part of a healthy identity) diminish in proportion to the handouts. There is no substitute for meaningful work in a stable setting. Motivation suffers considerable damage when one has been relegated to the periphery of society and its social and economic institutions. It is a vicious circle: lack of meaningful activity or work leads to more handouts, leads to more breakdown, leads to lesser motivation. Native people everywhere who have become victimized through culture contact tend to become less rather than more motivated to solve their identity problems. Native communities of welfare recipients tend therefore to perpetuate themselves on the periphery of the major cities or more covertly on the native reserves. The picture is the same all over the world.

How can motivation be changed? More handouts do not change it. All they do is keep the body and soul together but with no benefit to the soul. A return to the precontact situation is futile. One cannot set the clock back: eking out a nomadic existence has been given up for the easier life on welfare. The outstation movement will never restore the precontact identity of Aborigines, even as the white back-to-nature or back-to-the farm movements have never fully restored the sense of belonging at which the nostalgia was directed. The transistor radios, the schools, a permanently changed economic base have also changed irreversibly an entire world of meaning.

In history change has either destroyed a native race or the change has been absorbed in a new identity, providing fresh motivations and new activities. Change has never been successfully undone. This means that the only avenue or option open is the successful absorption of change. Yet for this sole remaining option a strange commodity is required. It is emotional energy. And it is precisely this emotional energy which change has drained out of the native population in particular or the destitute in general.

Even more important than the scarce commodity of "emotional energy" is the new identity configuration in which the changes have been absorbed or by which they have been "tamed." There must be a transcendental framework of order which meaningfully spans all experiences. Even as secular a movement as Alcoholics Anonymous stresses this transcendental order at the heart of its "creed." Yet it is Alcoholics Anonymous as against the far less successful welfare organizations which has restored motivation to the destitutes who had ruined themselves and their families through excessive drinking. Without exception these ex-alcoholics witness constantly to their changed identity and renewal of motivation as a "conversion" experience. However, this conversion would have been impossible had it not been for (1) the cohesion of the group which does the re-orienting and (2) the inexhaustible energy expended on guiding the potential convert out of his destitution into his new status. Traditional Aboriginal Society, as we have seen, used exactly the same techniques of emotional stripping and welding in its initiation ceremonies for adolescents and medicine-men.

The problem is not that such techniques are unknown in Aboriginal society, but that group or social identities of the required kind are scarce. There are few tightly knit groups which have come to terms with the enormous change brought about by Western contacts. This contrasts sharply with the various, well-documented revitalization movements of other countries in which Western/native elements merged smoothly and in which strong loyalties were purified by ascetic techniques.

In this study, the word "charismatic" has almost never been used in the actual descriptions. The one or two exceptions should be carefully noted. The Jinimin movement in Western Australia and Bandjalang Pentecostalism in Northern New South Wales are the only instances where charismatic leadership was mentioned. Only these two movements combined strong native leadership, anti-white sentiment, syncretistic beliefs, and ascetic techniques. The secular Don McLeod movement in Western Australia comes close to filling the bill, but Don McLeod is white and the belief-system is native (as far as I can gather) rather than syncretistic. Yet in other countries revitalization (or renewal of identity) movements have generally been successful only when these four characteristics were present: (1) leadership by charismatic figures who could strip away an old identity and weld a new one, because they were acquainted with, or could visualize both; (2) a strong anti-white, religiously motivated, and constantly reinforced stance; (3) a strongly held combination of traditional and Christian beliefs; and (4) a system of ascetic rules which would clarify all priorities and would give to beliefs position of place over the now-disciplined comforts of life.

This last point is important, because it leads indirectly to a reversal of the Aboriginal tradition since its contact with whites, to give economic security priority over maintenance of identity.

The importance of this point lies in the acceptance of the dichotomy between the economic (mastery) problem and identity. Although identity and religion can have important economic consequences, economic motivation in itself can have identity-destroying effects. Traditional Aboriginal society is a good example. The lure of becoming independent from the tyranny of nature was so great that Aboriginals were happy to surrender their way of life, their social organization, and their religion. They were fascinated by the European capacity to force nature to part with its fruits more copiously. Or better, they were fascinated by the end-products of that process, the consumer goods and agricultural produce. The jump to agricultural production was often too great to make.

Even now, after the genocidal consequences of exchanging one's heritage for a pottage of consumer goods have been uncovered for all to see, in their grim starkness, the Aborigine is very unlikely to return to the ancestral territory, unless the supply lines of modern conveniences and services are kept open. Ecological sentimentalism notwithstanding, the economic dragon still has to be appeased before the sacred territory will be inhabited again.

And yet taming the dragon means not letting him tame you first. One cannot tame what one is tamed by. What can he be tamed with? If Max Weber is correct, then the taming of the Western economy, so that it could develop in a capitalistic direction, could be brought about because the Puritan ascetic possessed the Archimedean point from which to manipulate it. So here too: one cannot tame the economic dragon if one is tamed by it first.

All this amounts to saying that identity and mastery may be at odds. The economic principle (to get maximum comfort for minimum effort) is less than neutral if it becomes the ultimate goal of existence. Then it tames, and by taming subverts. Economic mastery is ultimately inimical to stability because everything has to give for the sake of achieving the greatest comfort. The problem is not so much that the law of diminishing returns begins to operate, but that any change and any goal are ultimately justified by comforts.

We should not overstate our point. The Aborigines discovered soon enough that the price for greater independence from nature was the loss of identity and dignity. Therefore the present search is for the point of balance where alienation and anomie are at a minimum and economic security at a maximum. Or to say this differently: the search is for the point where change can be tamed sufficiently for identity to come into its own. Strangely enough this has always been a basic problem both before and after 1788, both for white and for black.

The alternative, to let the economic principle decide our goals for us, has proved to be an utter disaster for the Aboriginal and, more covertly, for the white man. There is actually not much difference between the level of identity and meaning problems in Australia between black and white.

The shoring of identity, therefore, is a way to tame the economic dragon. Aboriginal society solves none of its problems by amassing greater riches or larger budget allocations for Aboriginal Welfare. Not that a level of economic independence is not useful. Of course it is. Yet more important is the harnessing of the formless and the affirmation of that order which safeguards the totality of existence.

It is not likely that either wealth or The Dreaming in its old form will fill that bill. We have already said enough about the former. As for the latter, The Dreaming essentially represented an order in which nature reigned supreme. Only by artifical compartmentalization can this kind of objectified frame of reference be maintained next to a mundane existence in which this reign has obviously come to an end. The very function of objectification is the provision of multiple connections between it and the mundane, the one summing up what the other is about. An irrelevant frame of reference must soon erode into the multiplicity of half-baked commitments which crowd our age even as the sacred sites populated the clan's territory.

This conclusion is rather negative. We have said "no" to economic goals as ultimate (we could have added political power or scientific objectivity). We have also doubted the viability of The Dreaming (however sad this seems) for Aboriginality coming of age. And yet there are, both in The Dreaming and in Christianity (insofar as it is still taken seriously in the secular age which also claims to have come of age), numerous elements of dramatization, some of which come to the heart of things: wholeness/breakdown, salvation/sin, order/disorder, resurrection/crucification, life/death, and so forth. There is in both a basic commitment and loyalty, not to what man can control, but to what transcends man. There is in both a comprehensive intent that is abysmally missing in the segmented idolatries of the twentieth century.

It is in the affirmation of order in terms of some of these ingredients that the formless can be prevented from swallowing the firm.

Bibliography

BARWICK, DIANE. 1964. "The Self-conscious People of Melbourne." In Marie Reay (ed.), *Aborigines Now*, 20-31. Sydney: Angus and Robertson.

BATES, DAISY. 1947. *The Passing of the Aborigines*. London: John Murray.

BELL, JAMES. 1964. "Assimilation in New South Wales." In Marie Reay (ed.), *Aborigines Now*, 59-71. Sydney: Angus and Robertson.

BERNDT, CATHERINE H. 1961. "The Quest of Identity: The Case of Australian Aborigines." *Oceania* 32/2, 16-33.

BERNDT, RONALD M. 1951. *Kunapipi*. New York: International Universities Press.

————. 1965. "Law and Order in Aboriginal Australia." In Ronald M. Berndt and Catherine H. Berndt (eds.), *Aboriginal Man in Australia*, 167-206. Sydney: Angus and Robertson.

————. 1970a. "Introduction." In Ronald M. Berndt (ed.), *Australian Aboriginal Anthropology*, 1-18. Nedlands, W.A.: University of Western Australia Press.

————. 1970b. "Traditional Morality as Expressed Through the Medium of an Australian Aboriginal Religion." In Ronald M. Berndt (ed.), *Australian Aboriginal Anthropology*, 216-47. Nedlands, W.A.: University of Western Australia Press.

————. 1971. "The Concept of Protest within an Australian Aboriginal Context." In Ronald M. Berndt (ed.), *A Question of Choice*, 25-43. Nedlands, W. A.: University of Western Australia Press.

————. 1974. *Australian Aboriginal Religion*. Leiden: Brill.

————. 1976. "Territoriality and the Problem of Demarcating Sociocultural Space." In Nicolas Peterson (ed.), *Tribes and Boundaries in Australia*, 133-61. Canberra: Australian Institute of Aboriginal Studies.

————. 1977. "Aboriginal Identity: Reality or Mirage?" In Ronald M. Berndt (ed.), *Aborigines and Chance*, 1-12. Canberra: Australian Institute of Aboriginal Studies.

BERNDT, RONALD M., and CATHERINE H. BERNDT. 1970. "Some Points of Change in Western Australia." In Arnold R. Pilling and Richard A. Waterman (eds.), *Diprotodon to Detribalization*, 53-79. East Lansing: Michigan State University Press.

_____. 1977. *The World of the First Australians*. Sydney: Ure Smith.

BIRDSELL, J. B. 1970. "Local Group Composition among the Australian Aborigines: A Critique of the Evidence from Fieldwork Conducted since 1930." *Current Anthropology* 11/2, 115-42.

BLEAKLEY, J. W. 1961. *The Aborigines of Australia*. Brisbane: Jacaranda Press.

BROOM, LEONARD, and F. LANCASTER JONES. 1973. *A Blanket a Year*. Canberra: Australian National University Press.

BURRIDGE, KENELM. 1973. *Encountering Aborigines*. New York: Pergamon Press.

CALLEY, MALCOLM. 1964. "Pentecostalism among the Bandjalang." In Marie Reay (ed.), *Aborigines Now*, 48-58. Sydney: Angus and Robertson.

COLE, KEITH. 1977. "A Critical Appraisal of Anglican Mission Policy and Practice in Arnhem Land 1900-1939." In Ronald M. Berndt (ed.), *Aborigines and Chance*, 177-98. Canberra: Australian Institute of Aboriginal Studies.

CRAWFORD, I. M. 1968. *The Art of the Wandjina*. Melbourne: Oxford University Press.

DURKHEIM, EMILE. 1965. *The Elementary Forms of the Religious Life*. New York: Free Press.

ECKERMANN, ANNE-KATRIN. 1973. "Group Identity and Urban Aborigines." In Donald Tugby (ed.), *Aboriginal Identity in Contemporary Australian Society*, 27-41. Milton, Queensland: Jacaranda Press.

_____. 1977. "Group Organisation and Identity within an Urban Aboriginal Community." In Ronald M. Berndt (ed.), *Aborigines and Change*, 288-319. Canberra: Australian Institute of Aboriginal Studies.

ELIADE, MIRCEA. 1958. *Birth and Rebirth: The Religious Meanings of Initiation in Human Culture*. New York: Harper.

_____. 1973. *Australian Religions*. Ithaca, N. Y. Cornell University Press.

ELKIN, ADOLPHUS PETER. 1969. "Elements of Australian Aboriginal Philosophy." *Oceania* 40/2 (December), 85-98.

_____. 1974. *The Australian Aborigines*. Sydney: Angus and Robertson.

_____. 1977. *Aboriginal Men of High Degree*. St. Lucia, Queensland: University of Queensland Press.

FALKENBERG, JOHANNES. 1962. *Kin and Totem: Group Relations of Australian Aborigines in the Port Keats District*. Oslo: Oslo University Press.

FISK, E. K. 1975. *Policy Options in the Torres Strait*. Canberra, A.C.T.: Research School of Pacific Studies.

FRAZER, JAMES GEORGE. 1910. *Totemism and Exogamy*. 4 vols. London: Macmillan.

_____. 1937. *Totemica: A Supplement to Totemism and Exogamy*. London: Macmillan.

FREUD, SIGMUND. 1946. *Totem and Taboo*. New York: Random House.

GENNEP, ARNOLD VAN. 1920. *L'Etat actual du problème totémique*. Paris: Leroux.

GRAY, W. J. 1977. "Decentralisation Trends in Arnhem Land." In Ronald M. Berndt (ed.), *Aborigines and Change*, 114-23. Canberra: Australian Institute of Aboriginal Studies.

HALLAM, SYLVIA J. 1975. *Fire and Hearth: A Study of Aboriginal Usage and European Usurpation in South-Western Australia*. Canberra: Australian Institute of Aboriginal Studies.

HIATT, L. R. 1975a. "Introduction." In L. R. Hiatt (ed.), *Australian Aboriginal Mythology*, 1-23. Canberra: Australian Institute of Aboriginal Studies.

96   *The Firm and the Formless: Aboriginal Australia*

_____. 1975b. "Swallowing and Regurgitation in Australian Myth and Rite." In L. R. Hiatt (ed.), *Australian Aboriginal Mythology*, 143-62. Canberra: Australian Institute of Aboriginal Studies.

HOWITT, A. W. 1904. *The Native Tribes of South-East Australia*. London: Macmillan.

INGLIS, JUDY. 1964. "Dispersal of Aboriginal Families in South Australia 1860-1960." In Marie Reay (ed.), *Aborigines Now*, 115-32. Sydney: Angus and Robertson.

KABERRY, PHYLLIS M. 1939. *Aboriginal Woman*. London: Routledge.

KOLIG, ERICH. 1971. "Quo Vadis Australian Aboriginal Religion." *Bulletin no. 13*, 99-113. Vienna: International Committee on Urgent Anthropological and Ethnological Research.

_____. 1977. "From Tribesman to Citizen." In Ronald M. Berndt (ed.), *Aborigines and Change*, 33-53. Canberra: Australian Institute of Aboriginal Studies.

LANG, ANDREW. 1906. *Myth, Ritual and Religion*. London: Longmans, Green.

LÉVI-STRAUSS, CLAUDE. 1963. *Totemism*. Boston: Beacon Press.

_____. 1966. *The Savage Mind*. London: Weidenfeld and Nicolson.

_____. 1967. *Structural Anthropology*. Garden City, N.Y.: Doubleday.

LINTON, RALPH. 1924. "Totemism and the A.E.F." *American Anthropologist* 26, 296-300.

LOHE, M. 1977. "A Mission is Established." In Everard Leske (ed.), *Hermannsburg: A Vision and a Mission*, 6-41. Adelaide: Lutheran Publishing House.

LOMMEL, ANDREAS. 1969. *Fortschritt ins Nichts: Die Modernisierung der Primitiven Australiens*. Zürich: Atlantis.

LONG, J. P. M. 1970. "Change in an Aboriginal Community in Central Australia." In Arnold R. Pilling and Richard A. Waterman (eds.), *Diprotodon to Detribalization*, 318-32. East Lansing: Michigan State University Press.

MADDOCK, KENNETH. 1970. "Myths of the Acquisition of Fire in Northern and Eastern Australia." In Ronald M. Berndt (ed.), *Australian Aboriginal Anthropology*, 174-99. Nedlands, W. A.: University of Western Australian Press.

_____. 1972. *The Australian Aborigines*. London: Allen Lane, The Penguin Press.

_____. 1976. "Communication and Change in Mythology." In Nicolas Peterson (ed.), *Tribes and Boundaries in Australia*, 162-79. Canberra: Australian Institute of Aboriginal Studies.

_____. 1977. "Two Laws in One Community." In Ronald M. Berndt (ed.), *Aborigines and Change*, 13-32. Canberra: Australian Institute of Aboriginal Studies.

MALINOWSKI, BRONISLAW. 1954. *Magic, Science and Religion and Other Essays*. Garden City, N.Y.: Doubleday.

MATTHEWS, R. H. 1896. "The Burbung of the Wiradthuri Tribes." *The Journal of the Anthropological Institute* 25, 295-318.

_____. 1897. "The Keeparra Ceremony of Initiation." *The Journal of the Anthropological Institute* 26, 320-40.

_____. 1900. "The Walloonggurra Ceremony." *Proceedings and Transactions of the Royal Geographical Society of Australasia, Queensland* 15, 67-74.

_____. 1905. "Some Initiation Ceremonies of the Aborigines of Victoria." *Zeitschrift für Ethnologie* 6, 872-79.

_____. 1909. "Some Burial Customs of the Australian Aborigines." *Proceedings of the American Philosophical Society* 48/192, 313-18.
_____. 1911. "Initiation Ceremonies of Some Queensland Tribes." *Proceedings and Transactions of the Royal Geographical Society of Australasia, Queensland* 25, 103-18.
MCKEICH, ROBERT. 1977. "The Construction of a Part-Aboriginal World." In Ronald M. Berndt (ed.), *Aborigines and Change*, 252-65. Canberra: Australian Institute of Aboriginal Studies.
MCLAREN, JACK. 1926. *My Crowded Solitude*. London: Fisher Unwin.
MEGGITT, M. J. 1962. *Desert People: A Study of the Walbiri Aborigines of Central Australia*. Sydney: Angus and Robertson.
_____. 1966. *Gadjari among the Walbiri Aborigines of Central Australia*. Oceania Monographs 14. Sydney: University of Sydney.
MOL, JOHANNIS (HANS) J. 1976. *Identity and the Sacred*. Oxford: Blackwell, and Agincourt, Ontario: Book Society of Canada. New York: Free Press, 1977.
_____. 1982. *The Fixed and the Fickle: Religion and Identity in New Zealand*. Religion and Identity: Social-Scientific Studies in Religion 1. Waterloo, Ont.: Wilfrid Laurier University Press.
MOUNTFORD, CHARLES P. 1958. *The Tiwi: Their Art, Myth and Ceremony*. London: Phoenix.
_____. 1965. *The Dreamtime*. Adelaide: Rigby.
MOUNTFORD, C. P., and ALLISON HARVEY. 1941. "Women of the Adnjamatana Tribe of the Northern Flinders Ranges, South Australia." *Oceania* 12/2 (December), 155-62.
MUNN, NANCY. 1964. "Totemic Designs and Group Continuity in Walbiri Cosmology." In Marie Reay (ed.), *Aborigines Now*, 83-100. Sydney: Angus and Robertson.
_____. 1970. "The Transformation of Subjects into Objects in Walbiri and Pitjantjara Myth." In Ronald M. Berndt (ed.), *Australian Aboriginal Anthropology*, 141-63. Nedlands, W. A.: University of Western Australia Press.
PALMER, KINGSLEY, and CLANCY MCKENNA. 1978. *Somewhere between Black and White*. Melbourne: Macmillan.
PETERSON, NICOLAS. 1970. "Buluwandi: A Central Australian Ceremony for the Resolution of Conflict." In Ronald M. Berndt (ed.), *Australian Aboriginal Anthropology*, 200-215. Nedlands, W. A.: University of Western Australia Press.
PETRI, HELMUT. 1954. *Sterbende Welt in Nordwest-Australien*. Braunschweig: Limbach.
PETRI, HELMUT, and GISELA PETRI-ODERMANN. 1970. "Stability and Change: Present-day Historic Aspects among Australian Aborigines." In Ronald M. Berndt (ed.), *Australian Aboriginal Anthropology*, 248-76. Nedlands, W.A.: University of Western Australia Press.
RADCLIFFE-BROWN, A. R. 1926. "The Rainbow-Serpent Myth of Australia." *The Journal of the Royal Anthropological Institute* 56, 19-25.
_____. 1958. *Method in Social Anthropology*, Chicago: University of Chicago.
_____. 1961. *Structure and Function in Primitive Society*, London: Cohen and West. The section quoted in Chapter 1 was written in 1929.
ROWLEY, C. D. 1978. *A Matter of Justice*. Canberra: Australian National University Press.

SACKETT, LEE. 1977. "Liquor and the Law: Wiluna, Western Australia." In Ronald M. Berndt (ed.), *Aborigines and Change*, 90-99. Canberra: Australian Institute of Aboriginal Studies.

SMITH, PATSY ADAM. 1971. *No Tribesman*. Adelaide: Rigby.

SMYTH, R. BROUGH. 1878. *The Aborigines of Victoria*. 2 vols. Melbourne: Government Printer.

SOMMERLAD, ELIZABETH A. 1973. *Community Development at Hermannsburg: A Record of Changes in the Social Structure*. Canberra: Centre for Continuing Education, Australian National University.

SPENCER, BALDWIN. 1914. *Native Tribes of the Northern Territory of Australia*. London: Macmillan.

SPENCER, BALDWIN, and F. J. GILLEN. 1904. *The Northern Tribes of Central Australia*. London: Macmillan.

_____. 1912. *Across Australia*. 2 vols. London: Macmillan.

STANNER, WILLIAM E. H. 1965. "Religion, Totemism and Symbolism." In Ronald M. Berndt and Catherine H. Berndt (eds.), *Aboriginal Man in Australia*, 207-37. Sydney: Angus and Robertson.

_____. 1966. *On Aboriginal Religion*. Oceania Monographs, 11. Sydney: University of Sydney.

_____. 1968. *After the Dreaming*. 1968 Boyer Lectures. Sydney: Australian Broadcasting Commission.

_____. 1972. "The Dreaming." In William A. Lessa and Evon Z. Vogt (eds.), *Reader in Comparative Religion*, 269-277. New York: Harper & Row.

_____. 1976. *Some Aspects of Aboriginal Religion*. The Charles Strong Memorial Lecture. Canberra.

STREHLOW, T. G. H. 1964. "Personal Monototemism in a Polytotemic Community." In Eike Haberland, Meinhard Schuster, and Helmut Straube (eds.), *Festschrift für Ad. E. Jensen*, vol. 2, 723-52. Munich: Renner.

_____. 1968. *Aranda Traditions*. Melbourne: Melbourne University Press.

_____. 1970. "Geography and the Totemic Landscape in Central Australia." In Ronald M. Berndt (ed.), *Australian Aboriginal Anthropology*, 92-140. Nedlands, W.A.: University of Western Australia Press.

STURMER, J. VON. 1973. "Changing Aboriginal Identity in Cape York." In Donald Tugby (ed.), *Aboriginal Identity in Contemporary Australian Society*, 16-26. Milton, Queensland: Jacaranda Press.

TONKINSON, ROBERT. 1970. "Aboriginal Dream-Spirit Beliefs in a Contact Situation: Jigalong, Western Australia." In Ronald M. Berndt (ed.), *Australian Aboriginal Anthropology*, 277-91. Nedlands, W.A.: University of Western Australia Press.

_____. 1974. *The Jigalong Mob: Aboriginal Victors of the Desert Crusade*. Menlo Park, CA: Cummings.

_____. 1977. "Aboriginal Self-regulation and the New Regime." In Ronald M. Berndt (ed.), *Aborigines and Change*, 65-73. Canberra: Australian Institute of Aboriginal Studies.

_____. 1978. *The Mardudjara Aborigines*. New York: Rinehart and Winston.

TUGBY, DONALD. 1973. "Introduction: The Aboriginal Looking-Glass." In Donald Tugby (ed.), *Aboriginal Identity in Contemporary Australian Society*, 1-7. Milton, Queensland: Jacaranda Press.

WALLACE, NOEL M. 1975. "Living Sacred Sites." In Robert Edwards (ed.), *The Preservation of Australia's Aboriginal Heritage*, 125-27. Canberra: Australian Institute of Aboriginal Studies.

——————. 1977a. "Change in Spiritual and Ritual Life in Pitjantjatjara (Bidjandjadjara) Society, 1966 to 1973." In Ronald M. Berndt (ed.), *Aborigines and Change*, 74-89. Canberra: Australian Institute of Aboriginal Studies.

——————. 1977b. "Pitjantjatjara Decentralisation in North-West South Australia." In Ronald M. Berndt (ed.), *Aborigines and Change*, 124-35. Canberra: Australian Institute of Aboriginal Studies.

WARNER, W. LLOYD. 1964. *A Black Civilization*. New York: Harper & Row.

WATERMAN, RICHARD A., and PATRICIA PANYITY WATERMAN. 1970. "Directions of Culture Change in Aboriginal Arnhem Land." In Arnold R. Pilling and Richard A. Waterman (eds.), *Diprotodon to Detribalization*, 101-09. East Lansing: Michigan State University Press.

WENTWORTH, W. C. 1973. "Aboriginal Identity, Government and the Law." In Donald Tugby (ed.), *Aboriginal Identity in Contemporary Australian Society*, 7-15. Milton, Queensland: Jacaranda Press.

WHITE, ISOBEL M. 1975. "Sexual Conquest and Submission in the Myths of Central Australia." In L. R. Hiatt (ed.), *Australian Aboriginal Mythology*, 123-42. Canberra: Australian Institute of Aboriginal Studies.

WILSON, JOHN. 1970. "Assimilation, Acculturation, and the Emergent Subcultures." In Arnold R. Pilling and Richard A. Waterman (eds.), *Diprotodon to Detribalization*, 80-100. East Lansing: Michigan State University Press.

WILSON, KATRIN. 1970. "Pindan: A Preliminary Comment." In Arnold R. Pilling and Richard A. Waterman (eds.), *Diprotodon to Detribalization*, 333-46. East Lansing: Michigan State University Press.

WORMS, E. A. 1970. "Observations on the Mission Field of the Pallotine Fathers in North-West Australia." In Arnold R. Pilling and Richard A. Waterman (eds.), *Diprotodon to Detribalization*, 367-79. East Lansing: Michigan State University Press.

Index

Names

Subjects

liminality, 37
love, 26-27

marriage, 33-35, 75
meaninglessness, 37, 44
medicine man, 25, 91
missions, 73-78
moles, 6
morality, 50, 55-56
mummification, 42
myths, 5, 26, 46, 48-62

name, 43
nomadism, 65, 90

objectification, 5, 8-21, 39, 48, 93
opposition, 14-16, 41, 62
order, 44, 52-55, 93
outstations, 68, 90

parasitism, 65, 68, 88

rebirth, 37, 57-60, 88
religion, study of, 52-53
revitalization, 25, 63-82, 89, 91
rites of passage, 31-47
ritual, 2-3, 5, 14, 31-47, 51, 58, 68-69, 78, 82

sacralization, 5
sacrifice, 27, 29-30
salvation, 65, 75, 86, 93
sectarianism, 78-83
secularism, 83-86
sexuality, 12-13, 80
sky-being, 35, 51, 58, 61
snake, 25, 32, 57, 59, 62
sorcery, 25, 45-46, 88
soul, 43
stripping of identity, 31, 34-35, 41-44, 46, 75, 91
subincision, 38, 42, 67, 76
synchronic, 8

taboos, 22-24, 34-35, 43
taming, 91-93
territory, 2-3, 18, 49-52, 55, 68, 72, 82, 85, 87, 92
time, 65
tooth avulsion, 38, 42
totemism, 7, 9-12, 20, 31, 40, 45

water, 61-62
welding of identity, 31, 35, 38, 41-47, 75, 91
welfare, 89-90, 93
womb, 51

WESTMAR COLLEGE LIBRARY

DATE DUE

DEC 1 9 2012		

GAYLORD   #3522PI   Printed in USA